PR A

In this beautifully written book, Diana ....ad for those who yearn to receive the heart-to-heart messages our animal friends communicate to us for our own inner healing. Her keen sense of connecting with an animal's deep inner knowing results in educating her readers with humor, compassion and truth.

Michael Bernard Beckwith, author of *Life Visioning*

Diana opens windows to new ways of seeing our deepest interconnectedness with all animals and all that is. Her fascinating stories about human-animal communications open our hearts and minds to a more expansive appreciation of how we are all interdependent, and the opportunities we have to awaken and be of benefit to all beings. Read it, enjoy, learn, savor and share with others!

Allen M. Schoen, D.V.M., M.S., Ph.D (hon.), integrative veterinarian, teacher and author of *Kindred Spirits: How the Remarkable Bond Between Humans and Animals Can Change the Way We Live*

How many of us have washed ants down the sink? Reading this book puts life back into its proper place: life is a gift and we share the gift with more than our kind. Ms. DelMonte has brought her very special gift of animal communication and stories together to give the reader a wonderful access to this world which not many of us are privileged to visit or understand. She has written a marvel of a book! Every page is a story of compassion. Read this and be amazed and touched.

Phil Thompson, Bodhi Tree Bookstore former co-proprietor

Thich Nhat Hanh meets Dr. Doolittle in this collection of precise case studies of pets and their people. Diana DelMonte's captivating writing style combined with her accurate problems solving ability allows us all to learn from everyone's situations. This is a must-read for anyone who is connected to their pets.

Rachel Jones, D.V.M., C.V.C.P, holistic veterinarian

Diana DelMonte shares her personal experiences for many of the animals she has communicated with and helped over the years. She does this in a very readable and informative way that will help teach you to communicate and understand your own animal companions.

Charles Loops, D.V.M., homeopathic veterinarian

Diana DelMonte assists you in sensitizing yourself to the deep and rich world of communication with animals. You will discover oneness of all existence and enter into a world of love! This is a beautifully written and inspirational book.

Sandra Ingerman, M.A., author of *Soul Retrieval*
and *Medicine for the Earth*

I know from Diana's words, and the accuracy of her information after asking her to communicate with our dog Furphy cross country, that her work and book are an asset for all of us and an opportunity to expand our beliefs and our interactions with our animals.

from the foreword by Bernie Siegel, M.D.,
author of *Love, Medicine & Miracles and The Art of Healing*

In this book, Diana DelMonte discusses how animals often reflect our thoughts and emotions back to us, and she provides insights and perspectives about how to understand and communicate more deeply with our animals.

Gene Baur, best-selling author,
Farm Sanctuary president and co-founder

Why You Should

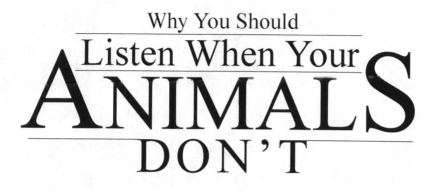

Listen When Your
ANIMALS
DON'T

How Your Animal's Behavior And Health Mirror Who You Are

DIANA DELMONTE

BALBOA
PRESS

A DIVISION OF HAY HOUSE

Cover and author photographs by Andy Stolarek www.furtographs.com

Edited by Pamela Guerrieri-Cangioli and Sandy Wanderman

Balboa Press books may be ordered through booksellers or by contacting:

Balboa Press
A Division of Hay House
1663 Liberty Drive
Bloomington, IN 47403
www.balboapress.com
1 (877) 407-4847

All the names of people and animals have been changed to honor the privacy of my clients.

Printed in the United States of America.

ISBN: 978-1-4525-2214-2 (sc)
ISBN: 978-1-4525-2215-9 (e)

Library of Congress Control Number: 2014916501

Balboa Press rev. date: 12/11/2014

For Jacob and Ryan
and for all the animals who have blessed my life.

CONTENTS

FOREWORD

Diana and I have lived the experiences she describes and have been changed by them. Years ago I did not believe in animal communication. It seemed nuts to me. But then my life was changed by what I experienced from my interactions with animal intuitives, and by my ability to communicate with animals once I understood how it was accomplished and followed their instructions.

It is by no accident that I became a surgeon, due to my past life experience, in which I killed with a sword. So, to make up for what I learned from that, our home has become a zoo. We rescued all types of creatures that needed a loving home, and I cure and heal with a knife now, rather than kill and injure.

As a four-year-old, I had a near death experience choking on a toy. I left my body and, as a child, I thought the ability to see and think while out of the body was an experience everyone knew about. When I didn't die, I was angry, because I felt disappointed to be back in my body again. For me, life is now a spiritual journey, and since animals are complete, while man is not, they have become my teachers.

I have learned to let experience be my teacher and to open my mind, just as Diana has done. I do not let beliefs block my ability to accept the truth. What taught me about the non-localization of consciousness, and the ability to communicate with all living things through it, was an event that happened several years ago. An indoor cat living at our son's house next door escaped when someone left the door open. It was essentially my cat living at his house. We live in a wooded area, and after several weeks there was no sign of the cat. I presumed she was dead. But I decided to challenge an animal intuitive I had met at an ASPCA non-kill conference in California. I sent Amelia Kinkade an e-mail asking her to find the cat... if she was still alive. Without even a photo of the cat, Amelia responded with an e-mail telling me she was alive, and that she could see the moon through my cat's eyes. She described our son's house in incredible detail and said that the cat was under the house. The "under the house" part made no sense to me until I found Boo Boo the next morning, hiding under a stairway with sides that came down to the ground. I brought her back into the house and fed and cared for her again. This story became a foreword for Amelia's first book.

This is why I wanted to write a foreword for this book—to awaken others to their abilities and to their potential to communicate, understand and rescue each other. The key I learned was similar to the message of a still pond. Diana emphasizes the importance of mindfulness, quieting the mind and using meditation, for your true reflection cannot be seen if the water is turbulent. If you want to communicate with animals, quiet your mind and stop the thinking part of your brain from making the decisions, because this is not about reason and logic, which can be completely wrong in some cases. The title of Diana's book says it all, and Helen Keller tells us that deafness is darker by far than blindness.

Here are some personal examples of my awakening from my experience with animal communication. One of my first was bringing our two dogs, Furphy and Buddy, to a training class to become animal communicators. I asked the students to tell me why our dogs urinated in the house. Their answer was that since we have so many plants in our house, they can't differentiate between indoors and outdoors. I laughed because that is so true about our home.

On another occasion, I scheduled an early morning veterinarian's appointment for two outdoor cats living at our son's house, knowing I could catch them when they showed up for breakfast and take them to the vet. Well, after I made the appointment, they didn't show up for a week. I called the vet and told him I was sorry to cancel. The morning after I cancelled the appointment, they both showed up for breakfast. Ultimately the vet let me give them their vaccinations since I was a doctor too. I have to trap our cats in a room in our house the day they know it's their day to visit the vet.

Several years ago, we rescued a rabbit named Smudge, and she became our house rabbit. She was free to roam the house and our fenced-in front yard. Every morning after her breakfast, she would run out through the pet door and spend the day in the yard with all our other creatures. I couldn't understand why she didn't come in when it grew dark, and when I tried to bring her in, she would run around the yard evading me for a prolonged and frustrating time. After I learned to live the message and to quiet my mind, I went out one evening and sent her my question: "Why don't you let me pick you up and bring you into the house?" I was startled by her answer and knew it was legitimate and not coming from my imagination. "You don't treat the cats that way."

I responded that I feared for her life if a predator climbed in at night, while I felt the cats were better able to protect themselves. After that conversation, the problem ceased except for the occasional evening when we both laughed as she teased me by running around for a minute.

The Bible speaks of everything God created, except man, as being good. A rabbi said the word *good* should be interpreted as *complete*. That is why I see animals as complete, and we have much to learn from them as we strive to become complete and use animals as our role models.

Just as each chapter in this book begins with a quote from which we can learn, so we can also see our animal's behavior as a quote to learn from. We are not their owners. We are their partners. If animals were not to be treasured and listened to, God would not have had Noah accept them all on the ark and instruct the Jews to feed the dogs while they wandered in the desert.

Animals provide us with many benefits through our relationship. Studies reveal how survival after life threatening events is higher for people who have pets than in homes with no pets. Animals change our body chemistry, help us to bond with one another, and they have shorter lives because they don't need all the time we do to learn about love and forgiveness.

Our cats Miracle and Hope know when I am in bed not feeling well. They come and sit on my chest and help me to heal. When I am resting, they join me to get some love and attention for themselves.

We feel for each other, and our animals intuitively know whether we are going to live or die, and they are able to warn us about impending medical emergencies. As Diana demonstrates, those animals close to us can also mirror our disease out of compassion.

When our dog Oscar was considered terminal by our vet due to cancer, I called the children to tell them we were going to euthanize Oscar. Over the phone they told me since I didn't euthanize my patients I couldn't do it to Oscar. So I brought him home, laid him down on the floor, and shared my love, massages, meals, and vitamins, and this terminal dog got up and was out the door in two weeks and lived for years with no sign of cancer. We have evidence now of the fact that the universal energy can be used to heal, and we are the battery cables which conduct it.

I'll never forget the dying cat that friends went to bring home from the vet after he called to tell them their cat was close to death. When the vet came out with the limp cat in his hands and the cat saw the family come in, the cat stood up on the vet's hands and leapt across the room onto the chest of a family member. The vet said, "Well, he was dying a few minutes ago." The cat was still alive a few years later.

Through my work with patient's dreams and drawings I know that we are aware of the collective consciousness and of the past, present and future. It is all a combination of what is behind creation—intelligent, loving, conscious energy.

My cat Miracle was named after a cat that appeared in a patient's dream. The cat announced, "My name is Miracle." Then she told the dreaming woman how to treat her cancer. The woman did, and is well today. I used my cat Miracle, from the time she was a kitten, as a therapy animal. She lived for over twenty years.

Our present dogs, Furphy and Buddy, come to all my support groups. Buddy intuitively sends me messages about how certain members of the group are doing while Furphy takes a nap and snores. His snoring, however, is therapeutic, because when people are sharing their tragic and life threatening situations and hear snoring, they get angry thinking we are falling sleep. We point out Furphy as the problem. Then they laugh, and their healing begins.

I know from Diana's words, and the accuracy of her information after asking her to communicate with our dog Furphy cross country, that her work and book are an asset for all of us and an opportunity to expand our beliefs and our interactions with our animals. It's hard for me to stop telling stories, but I will let you move on into Diana's book of wisdom and experience.

Bernie Siegel, M.D.,
author of Love, Medicine & Miracles
and The Art of Healing

ACKNOWLEDGMENTS

I would like to express gratitude to my animal companions, who have changed the direction and purpose of my life and who are responsible for my inward journey into healing, remote viewing, and telepathic communication. I first learned Reiki to help my own cats heal. I developed my telepathic skills to better understand my animals and to help others understand theirs. It is because of my animals that I practiced meditation—to sharpen my senses; to experience the quiet, expansive space that they do; and to be more present, as they are. They have been a continuous reminder of the Divine.

Through the years, I have learned feline etiquette: speak in the finest voice and step softly in the home. I thank all animals who have allowed me to talk to them, and those who have heightened my awareness and opened my heart. I have changed my diet for them and replaced my leather boots for more compassionate choices. It is my dream that, one day, all animals will be able to live decent lives, and will be revered, treated equally, and seen for the magnificent beings that they are.

I am also grateful to the humans in my life: to my brother Paul, who has more sense than anyone I know, and my sister-in-law Ruth, who has a heart of gold. Thank you for your support. Love and gratitude to my Father and Mother, who gave me this wonderful life, and to Lucy for her wisdom and belief in me. Thank you to those who provided amazing comments and feedback regarding their animals' sessions; their names will be kept anonymous. I'm grateful to have met Rosario who shared her dog Chico for the cover, and special thanks to Andy who photographed him and to Joy, his amazing assistant. Thank you to Pamela, Kim, Sandy and Rozanne for their marketing and editing expertise, and to Raymond Aaron—without his webinars, brilliant advice and generous thoughts I would still be mulling over the title.

Thank you, everyone.

LISTENING TO ANIMALS

Tuned in to the language
that goes beyond simple words,
feeling, forming a link
that allows all other than human
to take hold of a yowl
that calls us in.
Here we unite
with the undercurrent
and so listen to the wisdom
that swells forth always
from such fur and feather.

For Diana,
Sept 7, 2013
Jacqueline Suskin,
Poet, Los Angeles

Introduction

Everyone is a mirror image of yourself;
your own thinking coming back to you.
Byron Katie,
Loving What Is

There it was again. Sticky, walnut-brown residue streaked down my ex-boyfriend's twenty-inch face, as well as across the rest of my fine art photography and canvases leaning against the wall in my art studio. I had found this dribble down all the walls, audio speakers, and chair legs; now my metal art flat files were rusting and corroding from whatever this was.

I was clueless, until I caught my cat Bubby in the act—rather, until Bubby chose to make his demands clear as he raised his tail before my eyes. The look on his face was deliberate and direct as he struck the wall with a jet stream of urine.

Horror struck my face. Bubby meant business. No doubt about it. I wondered if he was being spiteful, or trying to ruin my career? It had never occurred to me that Bubby might have something to say.

Urination is communication. The location and consistency of the strike reveals the reason for this terrorist act, and also to whom in the household this message is aimed. Are we talking once a week? Every day? On the kitchen floor or on your bed? Pay attention. When you find piddle, from either your cat or dog, the point is always clear. Your animals are talking. Are you listening?

No?

Well then, CAN YOU HEAR ME NOW? This is when the tails rise.

Unfortunately, we often do not hear them or do not realize they are trying to communicate. We separate our animals from each other, tie them up, trade them in for others, isolate them from the family, ban them to the outdoors, give them away, dump them at the pound—or worst of all, we have them euthanized.

Our animals risk their lives for us. They beg to be heard. Getting rid of them is never a solution; it's just a Band-Aid on our wounds. Our unresolved emotions—those that our animals so sincerely and desperately want us to come to terms with—will continue to fester under our fortresses. Animals simply want us to look at ourselves... and perhaps give them a look, too.

This is why I became a translator for the animal kingdom—an animal communicator or "pet psychic," if you will—to bridge the wide gap between the human and animal species and to assist those who are already attuned and bonded with their animals and have a thirst and intention to understand their companions more. And I did it for those of you who are ready to understand yourselves in the process. Some people are not ready to take that step—and their animals' unacceptable behavior continues.

Animals often mirror our emotions and thoughts back to us through their behavior. We don't always acknowledge that an animal's behavior may be a reflection of us. Or maybe we do know, but we are not willing, or are too lazy, to gaze into the looking glass that they graciously hold for us. We have an opportunity to look at ourselves and a mission to change, if we choose to do so. We have the chance to learn about ourselves through our generous, kindhearted companions.

This is why animals come into our lives: to help us step up and see ourselves as the perfect beings that we are. They want us to be balanced and happy. They are here to teach us how to love ourselves and how to love unconditionally. Animals show by example through their unremitting kindness, forgiveness, and patience. They wait for humans to come around, to evolve into more loving and compassionate creatures. Animals are our spiritual companions. They are truly healers of the soul.

Animals are also empaths and naturally feel our true emotions. How do our animals feel when we are not honest with ourselves? When we argue? Each chapter in this book addresses a different aspect of when an animal's behavior, and sometimes their health, mirrors who we are. How do our animals tell us to pay attention to our surroundings or to our thoughts? How happy are our animals when we have not resolved our own issues or when we repress our emotions? How do they react to our thoughts about their death, and why do they sometimes leave home?

Most of the people who contact me to help them with their animals are already quite enlightened. No surprise. They are people who want to understand their animals in a deeper way. They know there is a soulful being under all that fur yearning to be heard and to express itself. And they want to know what their animals have to say.

It may surprise you to find how simple and natural the language of animals is, and to realize that telepathy is not a gift possessed by some, but it is our birthright and a natural ability possessed by all.

For those who doubt that telepathic communication is even possible, I have written this book especially for you. I cannot prove that I can hear an animal's thoughts, but I can share personal experiences that I have had "talking" to animals, and illustrate how an animal's behavior changes after engaging in a telepathic communication with them. You will see how and why this process is possible through the discoveries and progressive theories of modern science. All life is connected and communicating. Communicating with animals is the groundwork that makes communication with all life possible.

The case studies in this book demonstrate the wisdom, depth, and concerns of animals—both wild and domestic. The animals in these stories encourage us to follow our hearts. They have been profound catalysts for their humans' spiritual growth. There is Tiny, the Yorkie who alerted his human to her serious depression. Garfield, the cat who wouldn't stop scratching until his person learned to relax. Clea, the elderly Rottweiler who needed to reminisce before she could let go of life. Yudi, the cat who remembered an incarnation when he was a human. Pedro, the cat who left home to finally return after his person faced what she had been avoiding in her life. Dali, a dog who tore the house apart until his person learned to cope with her own anxious, addictive behaviors.

It is not uncommon to attract animals into our lives who can help us grow and evolve and help us see ourselves in a new light. We rescue animals who end up rescuing us. I believe we have soul contracts with everyone we meet on our life path—contracts that we make with each other and with the animals in our lives before we are born. There are no mistakes in the universe. We find each other lifetime after lifetime, teaching and learning from each other. Perhaps we agree, before we take a body, to the experiences and encounters that will shape our lives and that will give meaning and help us to evolve and grow—as painful as our experiences may be.

Some of our animal family members can exhibit challenging behaviors. The work we need to do on ourselves is humongous. Our animals are willing to sacrifice their comfort and even compromise their health to help guide us on our spiritual paths. Sometimes our lessons are tender and can bruise us for life. When is growing easy? Ram Dass says suffering is grace, necessary for spiritual growth. I believe that chaos brings Divine order to our lives. Blessings, disguised as challenges, provide opportunities for change and self-realization. Our animals are our best teachers and pave the way for us to follow.

Most of my clients know that we are all actors on a big stage, and that we all play a part in our dealings with one another on a higher level. There are no accidents and no one is to blame. Lisa understood this.

Devastated by the sudden death of her cat, Thomas, who was killed by a car, Lisa finally found healing through surrender and acceptance in knowing and believing in Divine purpose. She said Thomas' passing had brought her to me (our animals often lead us to people we need to meet and places where we need to be). She felt my words had pointed her to a mirror that reflected something she already knew in her heart.

This is what Lisa told me. "You have reminded me that I have a spiritual history that needs to resurface. I release Thomas to do his work, be it on me or someone else. I do hope he will return (rebirth). His presence is one of pure love. Thank you so very much—and I am thanking Thomas, as well as the driver, too—for bringing my attention around. I have much to do and many things to find solutions for or to eliminate from my life."

Yet the truth is, I had nothing to do with the solace Lisa found. Thomas did. It is by no accident or coincidence that our animals choose us and come into our lives. They also leave us in the manner that they choose. We all have a mission and a purpose in life and each other's life. We have soul contracts. Our helpers and guides may come in animal form. We should keep this in mind, to help us remember to cherish every living being.

The stories in this book will remind us to let go of guilt and blame, to practice mindfulness, to observe our mind states and to relax. You will see how listening to your animals deepens your relationship with them as well as with all life. And how dealing with an animal's passing can help us come to terms with our own mortality.

I invite you to read these stories with an open mind and heart. I hope that turning these pages will inspire you and change the way in which you see both your animal companions and yourself. I welcome you to the quantum world of Animal Communication.

My animals have raised my consciousness and changed my life's purpose and direction, from taking alcohol and drugs to teaching meditation and yoga. From skeptic to psychic. From artist to animal communicator—from painting my angst to writing books...about them.

Bubby sprayed the rooms and everything dear to us for nearly ten years—until my partner and I separated. After the problem was eliminated (us), and there was no more arguing and tension in the house, Bubby never struck again. Sometimes our lessons take a long time to learn. Who cares? We have until eternity.

Thank you, Bubby, for your patience, wisdom and empathy. I'm glad that I never even thought of getting rid of you. Need I say more?

Blessings For The Readers

On my website, www.DianaDelmonte.com, there are two blessings you can download that will enhance your relationship with your animal and reptile companions.

A detailed description of both the Zen meditation recording to train and quiet the mind, and the Kundalini Yoga meditation video to increase intuition, are explained at the end of the book.

Blessings,

Diana

CHAPTER 1

FROM SKEPTIC TO PSYCHIC—
WHY I TALK TO ANIMALS

Woo woo is where it's at.
Sonia Choqutte

I listen to animals because they have a lot to say, and because they speak truth. I talk to them because they listen. They care. They understand. They don't judge me. And because, sometimes, there's no one else around.

Nineteen years ago, my cat Bubby initiated me into the "woo woo" world of pet psychics. Good grief! I rolled my eyes when these people walked into the Bodhi Tree, a spiritual bookstore of World Religions located in West Hollywood where I had worked for several years—back in the day when I followed Holy paths damned seriously.

There was no room on my narrow road for animal talk. But Bubby, the gentle soul and avid sprayer, turned me around. It took him several tries to convince me. I was a self-absorbed artist who never wanted animals or any distraction in my life, let alone a talking cat. I only took in animals who begged at the doorstep and needed a home. Four-month-old Bubby was particularly insistent. He sat on a narrow window ledge on the second floor and stared at me painting. Every day.

My life with cats began at this point. It was a life of hugs and laughter, as well as cleaning poop and vomit, along with other extraordinary oozes—until Bubby shattered my world one Sunday afternoon.

It was a day as good as any. I had been writing at my drawing table that day when my pen ran out of ink. With my mind focused, relaxed, and still lost in what I had been writing, I strolled through the quiet house in search of another pen. As I approached the entrance of my partner's music room, a distinct voice shot through my mind. "Hey! Look out! I'm down here!" With eyes agape and a foot in midair, I saw Bubby lying across the threshold of the music room, glaring back at me. He had no intention of moving. Clearly, he had stopped me from trampling him by speaking to my mind. I passed it off as coincidence because, after all, animals do not talk.

Two months later, I sat with Bubby in the sunlight. My mind was focused in pin point attention, aware of only the warmth of his black, bushy, sunlit fur under the slow strokes of my hand. Just then, Bubby flashed me a vivid image of himself straining to urinate. Was he telling me he was having problems again? He had a history of urinary tract disease (FLUTD, a condition in which struvite crystals form in the urine and can create a life-threatening blockage). But I doubted myself. I did not take action or give the image a second thought. Two days later, Bubby had to be rushed to the vet for surgery.

After a third incident of animal communication, I became a believer. This time, it was my black cat, Yudi Boo Longfellow, who communicated to me in a dream. I'd had a hunch something was wrong with my plump, feline boy. I had asked Yudi if he was in pain. I heard nothing. So I asked him to please inform me somehow if he needed help. Then I went to sleep.

That night in a dream, Yudi showed me a thick soup surging through his body. When I awoke and asked Yudi if he were all right,

I heard an unexpected reply. "Take Baba Looie to the hospital." Baba Looie was Bubby's black, long-haired brother. Under Baba's skin, an unattended abscess had spread like thick soup across his entire upper back. Thanks to Yudi, I brought Baba to the vet in time.

It happened. I became a believer in the nutty world of animal communication. I found myself open to the possibility that maybe, just maybe, my animals were talking. Did Yudi know what a hospital was? Did cats know what an abscess was? Animals know when things are not right. They do not need words to define themselves or to convey their thoughts. They already have the foundation of communication: feelings and emotions. This is their language, conveyed telepathically. My job was to interpret their thoughts into my own words, like "abscess" and "hospital." Much like the way we interpret a human baby's screams and facial expressions. We are all mothers of intuition. Yet how do our animals communicate?

Animals Are Psychic

Animals think in pictures. They see your thoughts, or pictures, in your mind. This is why your animals wait by the door hours before you arrive home. They see the thought of home when it enters your mind. Biologist Rupert Sheldrake and author of *Dogs That Know When Their Owners Are Coming Home, And Other Unexplained Powers Of Animals,* did experiments disputing that animals merely respond to a conditioned routine.

In one of Sheldrake's experiments that spanned two years, a woman was transported in unfamiliar vehicles and taken to various locations. Cameras were installed in the woman's home to observe her dog's behavior. The woman returned in taxis, in other cars, by

3

bicycle, or she walked home. The time of her return was kept secret. Eleven minutes after the woman had been informed to return, her dog walked to the door to wait for her arrival. Animals are psychic.

I experimented with Yudi one day when he sat on the kitchen counter as I brewed a cup of tea. He loved to watch me cook; he even cried over chopped onions. Mentally, I asked Yudi to join me under the laurel tree while I held a picture in my mind of us both swinging in the hammock together. My round, sweet-smelling boy stared like an attentive friend as I "spoke" to him, and then jumped off the counter and ran away. Assuming my humble attempt at telepathic communication hadn't worked, I remained in the kitchen at least ten minutes longer. Finally, I grabbed a book and the steamy cup and headed outside. Much to my surprise, there was Yudi, waiting by the hammock and staring me straight in the face. Not only had he heard and understood me, but he hadn't forgotten.

Yet on that Sunday afternoon, Bubby had not sent me a picture. I had heard his *voice* at the entrance of the music room. Just as Yudi had heard my inner voice, I had heard Bubby's. How was this transference of thought possible? As a converted skeptic, I wanted to understand.

The New Science

The old school of Classic Physics believed the universe was held together by gravity and electromagnetic fields. In the new school of Quantum Physics, the universal field is thought to be held together by vibrating waves of energy, bouncing to and from each other in a boundless interplay of communication. Quantum physicists have proven that atoms and molecules everywhere are constantly exchanging information with one another. This is called the Zero Point Field because, even at a temperature of zero degrees, when activity normally stops, subatomic activity continues. All life is energy, connected and communicating. Even empty space is charged with energy.

During a silent Zen Buddhist meditation retreat at Mt. Baldy, we were asked to stare at an agave plant while contemplating the question: What is emptiness? For a long while, I saw nothing except the physical anatomy of the plant. However, as I unfocused my gaze a bit and continued to stare at the thick, pointed shoots, I perceived what I will describe as the plant's energetic imprint. I saw a replica of the plant, energetic shapes within and around each shoot—a vibrating, pulsing energy that was an integral part of the plant. It was the plant. It was the energy behind the form.

This is what Buddhists have been chanting in the Heart Sutra for 2,500 years:

Form is No Other Than Emptiness. Emptiness is No Other Than Form.

Perhaps those who still feel an amputated leg are feeling the energy blueprint of the leg. Photons, small units of light, bounce constantly to and from our bodies. We are more than muscle, blood and bone. We are energy and light and are made up of ninety-nine percent space.

We live in a holographic universe, physicists say, because we are part of the larger whole. We are not separate from, but contained within, this cosmic web, joined with one another and with all that exists, even at a distance. How else could I communicate to a dog across the country, locate a missing animal in Peru, or send healing to a woman in Brazil? The Brazilian woman had felt tingling and warmth spreading through her belly—exactly the place where I sent the healing energy. I hadn't told her this, and she had forgotten to mention beforehand that she was having stomach issues. The energy knew where to go and was felt more than 5,000 miles away.

Thoughts are energy and travel faster than the speed of light. We are a part of the Quantum Field, the Divine Matrix or the Creative Intelligence pervading all that is. God. Source Energy. Buddhists call it Mind. Everyone has a different word to describe this unified field of awareness. In his book, *Remote Viewing*, David Morehouse writes: "The Matrix Field has been described as a huge, nonmaterial, highly structured, mentally accessible framework of information containing all data pertaining to everything in both the physical and non physical universe."

Telepathy is the universal language and link between all species, because it is the innate, Divine intelligence that resides deep within all life. Telepathic communication transcends race, species, geographical location, and even death. It is truly the language of the future.

The Good News Is...We Are All Psychic

Do you see the clothes you intend to wear in your mind's eye? Do you ever visually recall where you left your car keys or imagine what you plan to eat for lunch? Telepathy is our natural language. It is so natural that we are not even aware we use it in our everyday interactions with one another. We do more than listen to each other. We receive information by watching another's facial expressions, eyes, and body posture. We also visualize what we want to attract or manifest in our lives. Visualization is the basis for all creation. Therefore, all of us are clairvoyant. *Clair* is French for clear. *Voyant* means seeing. *Clear seeing* is seeing that goes beyond the physical eyes.

When we feel another's pain, embarrassment, pride, or joy we are clairsentient, or *clear feeling*. Gut feelings are always correct. Our bodies never lie. They are like huge antennae, gathering information without our conscious awareness. The navel center, or Nabi chakra, is the power center and seat of our emotions and can be considered the third brain.

We are clairaudient, which means *clear hearing*. We intuit what is not said by the inflection and tone of another's voice. Our inner voice speaks to us and guides us. When we don't listen, we can find ourselves in a jam. The quieter our minds become, the louder and clearer the inner voice. The more we learn to trust it, the stronger it becomes.

Every one of us has felt inspired, has had sudden realizations, has thought or dreamt of someone who shows up or calls the next day. There are times when we just know when to take action or know what is best for us. Although we do not know *how* we know, we process the information in a split second and trust it. We have tapped into the Divine Intelligence within, or *clear knowing*: claircognizance.

These layers of information stream in simultaneously when I communicate to animals. While sensing the energy and intention behind the information, I stay aware of verbal thoughts, images in my mind, sensations in the body, and feelings in my gut. I never doubt that spontaneous knowing. Animal communication is a holistic, subtle language.

Owen Waters, author of *Telepathy and Animals*, referred to this transference as "thought balls" because a single image can hold an entire story. A single picture can be delivered with feelings, emotions, and intentions, and sometimes with sounds, smells and taste.

While teaching a remote Animal Communication class, working from photographs of the participants' animals, I instructed the class to begin by simply looking at their animal photo. Just then, I remembered Andrea, a sixteen-year-old student in the class, was blind. I added, "Or have someone describe the animal to you." Sensing energy without a

7

photo can take years of practice. Andrea had already missed the first half of instruction, and I feared that she would feel lost and frustrated. Immediately, I followed up. "If you feel stuck then just imagine you are talking to the animal. Have fun with it."

I was blown away. Andrea picked up accurate information about the animal just by knowing the animal's name and physical description. It was her first time taking an introductory animal communication workshop. Afterwards, Andrea hugged me. With tears in her eyes, she said, "Oh, thank you so much. I never thought I could do this. I never thought it was possible to talk to an animal, or that it was all in the imagination... and that the imagination was real!"

I had never thought about the telepathic process quite like this before. The mechanics of telepathy, connecting to an animal, and sending and receiving thoughts is all in the imagination. What else is there? The imagination is a boundless universe full of possibilities waiting to be realized.

Matter is energy vibrating at a slower frequency. All of us can fine tune our antennae to the higher frequencies to hear, see, send and receive information to and from the Quantum Field. We have the most sophisticated, advanced technology right inside our own heads. Author and visionary, Gregg Braden, says external technology is only a manifestation of the technology already inside ourselves—a technology waiting to sprout. We cannot create anything that does not already exist within. Creation begins from the inside out.

Animals have a heightened awareness and sensitivity, because they are not dependent on words. They sense our intentions and energy, feel our emotions and see our thoughts. When you throw your thoughts around, your animals catch the whole "ball" and sometimes throw it back to you. They know you more than you know yourself.

I interpret an animal's feelings, emotions, and thoughts and translate the information into words for you. I imagine my consciousness reaching the animal and connecting through the heart center.

Our awareness is not confined inside our heads. It expands throughout and even outside our bodies, and we can consciously expand it further. The heart has a magnetic field thousands of times bigger and more powerful than the brain and is considered the second brain.

Animal communication is a heart-centered language. Although animals function through the lower three chakras[1]—through instinct, survival, power, and connection to the physical—they primarily operate from the higher centers, including the heart and third eye center, through telepathy, intuition, and compassion. Animals are highly evolved.

The Dogs And The Boss

Animal communication works. I worked in an upscale doggy day care center for one month. I was thrown into the job of washing, grooming and trimming the toenails of dogs. I had absolutely no idea what I was doing. I didn't even have dogs. I relied on my telepathic abilities to get the dogs to cooperate. One dog in particular, a long- nosed, massive-haired Collie as tall as my chest, would not get up into the bath area. I certainly could not lift him! After several timid attempts, I mentally asked the Collie to please help me out, since I could not do this without his cooperation. I think I might have begged him. He climbed right in.

Then there was the dog who had viciously attacked another and was put in a cage for time out. After several hours, the staff thought it was

---

[1]   The chakras are sacred centers, spiritual energy vortices located along the spine that correlate to levels of consciousness and organs in the body. They reflect our mental state, influence our emotional life, and affect our physical health.

fine to release him. I warned them not to! I had already talked to the dog in the cage who, still angry, told me he would kill that other dog if he got out. They rolled their eyes, released the dog, and all hell broke loose.

I quit. This is why. I had no experience in handling a pack of dogs. Every day I opened the inside gate of the two-thousand square foot cement warehouse and was stampeded by at least forty large, assorted dogs, including both mutts and powerful Pit Bulls, Rottweilers, Mastiffs and Great Danes. I was greeted by Boxers, Dobermans, Old English Bulldogs, and that big Collie—all barking, howling, and pressing their noses against my body and trampling each other to possess me.

My job, bedsides mopping urine off the floor with bleach every five minutes, was to be ready in case a fight broke out. When one did, I was expected to grab both dogs by their collars, pull them apart, and kick one of them in the head. Not to worry, I was directed—it won't hurt them. They have thick skulls. I wasn't very good at this. In fact, I froze in place while two dogs nearly killed each other and was then shoved aside by a trim, tall, dog dominatrix who did the job right. I knew that I would never be able to kick any animal in the head, no matter how thick their skull. That was the end of that job.

However, here is the interesting observation I made during my short time working there. Except for an occasional brawl, the dogs were calm and playful. They got along until the owner of the business walked in the building. I always knew when she arrived because the dogs acted out. They became agitated, aggressive and vocal. I didn't have many dealings with the owner myself. I found her to be distant, cold, surly and argumentative. The dogs felt her energy when her car pulled up, and a fight would break out.

Animals mirror our emotions. Sometimes, resolving problems involves looking at ourselves.

Chapter 2

Being Honest With Animals— And With Yourself

The language of the body is emotions.
The language of the Spirit is pictures.

John Fulton,
healer, Los Angeles

Even though your animals can see your thoughts, they need to be told what's going on. It's not enough to tell a human friend that you are leaving. They want to know when, where you are going, how long you'll be gone and when you'll return. It is no different with your animals. Talk to them!

Monkey in the Bedroom

Sally called me because her bulldog, Monkey, was pooping in her bedroom. He didn't make a mess in any other room in the house—just the bedroom. Undoubtedly, Monkey had something to say to Sally.

Monkey told me he did not want to be left alone. Sally had no idea what this meant. She and her husband never left Monkey alone.

She worked at home. Monkey was their baby, and they would never think of leaving him by himself. I did another session with Monkey. Again, I heard, "I don't want to be left alone." Surely, I was missing something or was not interpreting his thoughts correctly.

I did a third session with Monkey and explained to him that Sally would never leave him alone. He had nothing to worry about. Entering his body with his permission, I did an energetic body scan, or internal viewing, and found nothing wrong with his organs. Monkey was a healthy dog. I asked him why he continued to poop on the rug.

For the third time, I heard the same thing. I suggested Sally call another communicator. There was nothing more I could do. I was stumped, and Monkey continued to poop in the bedroom.

Before we hung up, Sally and I chatted about our lives. She said she was disappointed. She had wanted to clear this issue up before she and her husband left for vacation.

"VACATION? Have you told Monkey?"

It had never dawned on Sally that Monkey had heard them discussing their plans, nor had she ever thought of informing her dog! I explained to Monkey when his beloved people would be leaving, where they were going, when they would return and who would be feeding him. Monkey stopped leaving deposits on the bedroom carpet.

How Dare You Leave Me!

When Viola returned from vacation her cat, Skeeter, ignored her and refused to come into the house. Sometimes, he would leave for a few days. Skeeter was upset at Viola for not telling him when she was leaving and when she would return. This created so much anxiety for Skeeter that he was simply pissed off at Viola when she finally did return.

Always tell your companions when you will return, even when you leave for work. Never assume they are familiar with your routine or that they accept it. You can send them a mental picture of you leaving when the windows are light (daytime) and returning when the windows are dark or dim (night time). You could also send an image of the sun or the moon. This conveys one day. Do this for as many days as you will be gone. If you are leaving for one month, mentally show them seven days and then imagine this block of time again to represent the second week and again for the third week, etc. The concept may seem abstract, but our animals get it. To indicate the day you will return, send them the picture of you entering the house with a big smile across your face and all of you together again. This is important. They need to know you're coming back, and this mental image caps the time frame.

Za Za Fabiana

A small-framed, graceful Italian Greyhound named Za Za urinated on the living room carpets, the kitchen floor and the upstairs hallway. I knew Megan and Michael spent quality time with Za Za and always took her for long walks, yet I sensed a disconnect here with a family member. Her heart center was off balance. All Za Za told me was that Megan's son had treated her like a special girl. And then she asked, "Why can't I go into his room?" Afterwards, Megan told me she kept her son's door closed while he was away at college. I told Meagan that Za Za missed him terribly and that perhaps Za Za wished to see his room for herself or smell his scent. Megan explained to Za Za why her son had left and when he would return. She now left her son's bedroom door open for Za Za, who stopped urinating all over the house.

Please Stay Together

Savanna had been peeing all over the house for six months when Alison finally called me. Among the three cats, Savanna was the one who voiced her opinion. Just as in the human realm, there are some of us who let things slide, and some of us who refuse to ignore unpleasant circumstances. Since Savanna mostly targeted the bedroom carpet directly in front of Alison's dresser, I suspected this had to do with Alison.

Savanna's heart chakra was off balance. She told me, "Alison is divided. She isn't whole anymore." Savanna showed me an empty house and said, "Everyone's gone. Alison is thinking of selling the house. I don't want to move. I want things to be the same as before." Since Alison's heart center was also off balance, I asked her if she was grieving, and if she was thinking of selling the house.

Alison was not thinking of selling the house, but she and her husband were going through a divorce. Alison was grieving the end of her marriage. Her husband had moved out six months ago. Now that Alison filled me in, I could explain to Savanna why things were different now. I could reassure Savanna that she would not be moving, and that Enrico, Alison's husband, would always come by to visit her.

Immediately after the initial session with Savanna, when I had only gathered this information from her, and before I explained anything to her, she began to interact more with Alison. She only peed once that day, instead of several times. Simply having the opportunity to be heard and acknowledged is sometimes enough. Now I would continue my work with Savanna, until she agreed to use her box.

A Pact With The Pigeons

I lied to the birds. Pigeons. Nesting on the wooden rafters under the roof, directly above my back door. I had to leap two feet to enter and leave my apartment, because they splattered their poop all over the cement landing. When I hosed down the area, the poop quickly piled up again. The owners agreed to have spikes installed in the rafters to discourage the birds from gathering. But the pigeons returned and huddled between the spikes.

I decided to make a deal with the birds. I projected my thoughts to them; I would give them food if they would kindly make their nest elsewhere. They left the next day. For one month they waited patiently for me to complete my end of the bargain. I never did. I was busy teaching children at a summer camp, and I simply forgot. Droppings appeared on the step again.

Then one day as I got into my car and began driving down the road, I noticed a pigeon, two rooftops away across the street, looking at me. The bird swooped down, flew to my moving car and hovered over the windshield as I was driving. He looked me in the eye, and I heard his thoughts clearly. "Where's the food?" I finally kept my promise. I threw bread and seeds in my back yard, and I never found poop on my back step again.

Always keep your word. Never con your animals. It just doesn't work.

Too Many Rules!

Nancy had just moved in with her boyfriend. This was quite an adjustment for her cats Morley and Sawyer, who had lived alone with Nancy since kitten-hood. Morley became aggressive, biting and hissing. He stopped using his box. Since he soiled in the same spot, and never in front of Nancy, there was a good chance that this was not aimed at Nancy personally but was a reaction to a dynamic in the household. One thing was for certain: Morley was angry and demanded answers.

Beginning the session with a body scan, I slipped into Morley's body and took a look around while remaining aware of feelings, energy blockages, and sensations felt in my own body—a mirror now of his body. If an aggression or a urination problem continues after a communication session, I always advise a trip to the vet. I never diagnose. I only know what the animal feels, what s/he tells me, and what I see or feel during my internal viewing.

I found nothing wrong with Morley, so I asked him what was going on.

He hit me with this. "Things aren't fair! All these rules!"

"Are you upset with Nancy, Morley?" I asked.

"No. She means well, but I have to always fight for her attention. Sawyer is always in her face!" (I learned later that Sawyer had taken Morley's position on Nancy's pillow in bed.)

"Are you upset with Nancy's boyfriend?"

"No, but I wish he were around more."

"So who's making all the rules, Morley?"

"Nancy. I liked the old routine."

"What was that, Morley?"

"Waking up with Nancy. We had more of her time. They don't want us on the counters anymore! And there's no smoking!"

"Is there anything you would like Nancy to know, Morley?"

"She needn't pretend she's happy when she's not. We know how she's feeling. There's been tension building up around here!"

Nancy laughed. The inflection in my voice matched Morley's personality, she said, and it was all true. She was no longer as carefree as she had been. Her boyfriend was gone for long stretches at a time, and Nancy had more responsibility. Before the move, she had spent mornings lingering with her cats in bed. Now she rose early but had less time. Tension had built up over the fact that her boyfriend did not want the cats on the counters anymore. The boyfriend was indeed a smoker, and Nancy had banned smoking in the house. Morley felt the conflict and tension mounting over these matters.

Nancy said she would try to spend more quality time with her boys, and I explained to Morley and Sawyer why things were different now. Cats do not like change and, just as we do, they need adjustment time.

Get Out Of My House!

We often forget to inform our animals of changes or surprises, so they know what to expect. We assume they will figure out whatever it is that we are not telling them. I got an emergency call one evening from a desperate pet sitter who had to enter Murray's house the next morning to feed him and change his litter box. Murray, a handsome, brown tabby feline, had a reputation of being unfriendly to humans. He would not let the pet sitter into his house on the first day, nor would he let anyone enter his home. He lunged at people, and sometimes attacked and bit his own person. I didn't know if I could make any progress with Murray overnight, but I had to try. When I asked Murray how he felt when others entered his home, I felt as if I was suffocating. I knew this was not physical but was how fear felt in Murray's body. This big, ferocious bully was terrified of people, and feeling vulnerable, he went into panic mode. I explained to Murray who the pet sitter was and what her loving intentions were. I promised Murray that she would not only keep her hands to herself but would stay a good distance away from him. However, I explained, he had to allow her to do her job. I told Murray to sit high and let her pass. The very next day, the pet sitter called to say Murray had just watched her the entire time, allowed her to pass by him to do her duties, and never hissed or budged from his window seat. Even when animals know your intentions, their fear can override their good judgment.

I understood why Murray felt so vulnerable when I later learned he had been declawed. A cat's claws are not only used for defense, but are also needed for grooming, stretching and expressing affection. Some people believe that declawing is a simple surgery that removes a cat's nails in the same way you would have your fingernails trimmed. But it involves the amputation of the last bone of each claw, cutting through bone, tendons, skin and nerves, and would be similar to cutting each of your fingers at the last knuckle. Not only does this procedure cause back pain, arthritis and lameness, it also presents lifetime emotional problems for the cat. This cruel practice has been banned in many countries. It has been banned in West Hollywood, California.

Let's Stay Home

Remember that your animals are sensitive. They love and teach us about ourselves. They allow us to take baby steps, and they try to protect us from our darkest, deepest, best-kept secrets and fears.

Roberto asked me if his brown and white Pit Bull, Lulu, would tell me why she would not go for walks. What dog wouldn't enjoy exploring the neighborhood and spending quality time with their person? But Roberto said that after they would walk about twenty feet, Lulu stopped and refused to budge one step further.

Immediately, I heard the word "allegiance." I had a hunch and asked Roberto if he enjoyed walking. He answered that, in fact, he did not like walking around his neighborhood. He only did it for his dogs. The neighborhood was not safe, and Roberto did not feel secure.

The dog had felt her person's resistance and fears and understood his boundaries. Lulu had no intentions of making Roberto do anything that made him uncomfortable. She sacrificed her walk to do him a favor.

Lead With Joy

Natalia was not surprised to find pee and poop on the rugs in her house when she came home from work. Her dog Mickey had been soiling since she brought him home one year ago. Mickey not only did this when she was gone, but also immediately after they returned from a walk, even though he was given plenty of time outside to do his business. He also often waited until Natalia was looking right at him. This was obviously targeted toward Natalia.

Mickey was a handsome long haired fellow, mostly black with tan legs, muzzle and eyebrows and big, frank, dark eyes. He had a rebellious spirit and either ran away every chance he got or refused to come back when called. Natalia had once lost him for two days. She wondered what was on her dog's mind.

Looking at his photograph I immediately sensed that Mickey wasn't grounded, and that there was a power struggle between him and his person. He was a smart dog who needed a purpose in his life. He had no structure, and like a young teenager, he needed boundaries and direction. He said that he and Julio, Natalia's Boxer, were a team. He felt that Julio needed a little leadership, and said, "That's where I come in. I teach him things."

Like what?

"Like how to be seen and heard around here."

Natalia confirmed this and said that, despite being a small dog, Mickey was the alpha and had taught Julio how to escape through the fence. I could feel Mickey's determination and demands. He was

19

trying to control Natalia. I asked him why he ran away all the time. He showed me his life in a former home living with an elderly woman who didn't let him out much.

Mickey told me, "I want to see the world. Natalia worries too much. She holds my leash too tight. She is always afraid. Tense. Sometimes I want to break away and have fun. This is what Natalia needs to do. She needs to listen to me. Tell her to take charge, but in a gentle way. Lead with joy."

Natalia disagreed. She said she was an extremely joyful person, and she did not hold the leash too tight, but that Mickey wore a choke chain. When he pulled, it hurt his neck and he would cry. Why did a small dog, the size of a Chihuahua, need to wear a choke chain?

"Because," Natalia said, "Mickey is an escape artist who squiggles out of every collar and harness he has ever worn." Natalia was afraid of losing him again.

The following day after my session with him, Natalia called to say that when she took the dogs out for their walk, Mickey urinated right on her shoe.

Apparently, Mickey's feelings still had not been heard, and I needed to peel away more layers. Natalia then mentioned that Mickey was kept in a crate all day—ten to twelve long hours. He had been confined like this every day for the past five months now. I explained to Natalia that we could not possibly gauge our progress if Mickey was kept in a crate, and that if she expected me to help him, she needed to let him out and take her chances. She said she could not do that, because whenever Mickey was out of his crate he destroyed the house.

What? Why had Natalia left out this important information? What exactly had this tiny dog done?

"He has ripped holes in the couch, torn the rugs up, scratched the woodwork, tattered the curtains, chewed my credit cards and my shoes."

"Oh?" I asked, "and this just slipped your mind?"

Now I needed to start again, and take a long look at Natalia, not just her dog. I suggested to Natalia that if she was not ready to trust Mickey and uncrate him, then to consider confining him to the kitchen during the day, or any room where he could not do too much damage, but where he could at least have space to stretch his legs.

"Well, I cannot do that," Natalia said, apparently forgetting to mention another minor detail. "If Mickey is not crated, he bites the dog walker."

Natalia! Is there anything ELSE I need to know?"

Natalia finally gave me the full picture. Her dog was out of control. After addressing each issue with Mickey, the wild child, and looking at the chakras involved that motivated each of Mickey's behaviors, as well as looking at the emotional centers in Natalia that related to each issue, I found four chakras that were consistently off balance in both of them: the throat, heart and the lower two centers.

Natalia was gone for too long. Mickey told me, "When she returns from work, she keeps herself busy. She doesn't have enough time for herself. She won't let go."

Natalia agreed. When she returned home from a twelve hour work day, she buried herself in front of the computer until it was time for bed.

Was Natalia the truly joyful person that she claimed to be? As I probed, I realized that Mickey's comments about his person were both literal and figurative. Natalia was tight, not only with Mickey's leash, but with her own life as well. Tony wanted her to take charge of him, as well as to take charge of her own life, but in a gentle way. Her own life felt out of control, and she had difficulty letting go, trusting and leading with joy.

I asked Natalia which parts of her life left her feeling frazzled and falling apart? She said she was worried about finances. She had recently purchased a home, and her design business was slow. These were all lower chakra issues (finances, foundation, security, fear) which created stress for Natalia, a self-employed, single woman with a mortgage. Like Mickey, perhaps Natalia needed to "break away and have fun."

Then the throat and heart centers needed to be addressed. Natalia didn't appear to be lonely, so I asked, "Has anyone close to you died recently? What are you angry about? And who have you not been expressing your feelings to?"

Natalia then told me she was still grieving the loss of her dog, Lizzy, who had passed away shortly before Mickey came into the household. Mickey could see Lizzy in Natalia's thoughts, and he could feel Natalia's sadness. Mickey needed to know the full story. She needed to tell him about Lizzy. Natalia also needed to talk to Lizzy, and tell her departed dog whatever it was that she had been holding back. Our animals who are in spirit, and our human loved ones who have died, are still with us and can hear us.

Natalia talked to Mickey, and even showed Mickey Lizzy's picture. Then she cried and talked to Lizzy. She now took time for her dogs, and everyday she told them where she was headed and when she planned to return. She released Mickey from the crate, and trusted that all would be fine. While at work, she held this optimistic feeling inside her as well as the mental picture of a clean and orderly house, instead of anticipating a mess when she walked into her home. After work, she spent time relaxing on the couch with both Julio and Mickey.

I gave Mickey three jobs; to get the mail with Natalia each day (his idea, not mine), to greet people and to keep the house clean. I told him to greet the dog walker. She was there to have fun, and that he didn't need to hide under the bed or bite her when she came too close. I told him he had a choice, and that he did not have to go walking if he did not want to.

Sending Mickey healing energy to relax him, I also sent energy to ground him, so he would feel solid and secure in his body. I imagined a golden cord radiating from him and attaching to Natalia, to give him the feeling of safety and connection to his person, no matter how far away she physically was. I surrounded him within an imaginary bubble of white light so he felt protected. I spiritually aligned him by imagining another golden cord rising from his crown chakra to the Creator.

Then I did several rounds of the Emotional Freedom Technique (EFT)[2], for both Natalia and Mickey, as I tapped the meridians on my body—a surrogate for their bodies, since they were located clear across the country—while addressing the emotional concerns associated with those particular chakras.

The dog-walker reported that Mickey has been in a good mood and easy to handle. Mickey has chosen to go for his walks and no longer tries to bite her. Since the dog walker began telling Mickey where they were going, and that they would return, he no longer looks back toward the house like he used to. He has not chewed one single thing, keeps the house clean and doesn't use his home as a bathroom. Mickey has complete freedom in the house now and is no longer crated. Soon Natalia will walk him with a harness and leash, instead of a choke chain.

---

[2] EFT or Emotional Freedom Technique, is a process that involves tapping specific meridians in the body, while verbally repeating statements to release trauma or negative habitual thought patterns and emotions. www.emofree.com or www.thetappingsolution.com

When I had started working with Natalia, I felt resistance. She seemed to discount every insight that I had shared with her. She wasn't ready to be honest with herself. She had not worked through her grief. She was overwhelmed with her workload and had not realized it. Natalia worried, did not trust herself and was too afraid to let Mickey out of the crate. It was easier to keep her dog under control than to keep an eye on her own life.

After she listened to what Mickey had to say about her, she felt a shift inside. Natalia was willing to let go of those things she could not control. She acknowledged her fear and stress, and then began to trust me, her dogs and the process of her life. When she finally set an intention and announced, "We can do this!", Mickey's behavior changed.

The Red Broom

Our human minds run like wild horses, projecting into the future or reflecting the past. Animals live mostly in the present moment. But this is not to say that animals don't remember their past or worry about the unknown. They do, especially with a traumatic past.

Chris wanted to know why his full-grown Doberman, Jake, paced back and forth in the car. Layers of issues related to Jake's anxiety, and it took much probing to get to the root cause—not probing of the dog, who was clear from the start, but of Chris, who I sensed was holding back information.

Jake was a big dog who was left alone for long hours in a small apartment. This would be like a human spending the entire day in a bathroom. Jake told me Chris was never home. (Chris worked all day and then went to the gym.) Jake showed me that Chris was often anxious and in a scattered rush at home. When Chris took Jake to the park, he blasted his car radio and his mind was elsewhere. All of this contributed to Jake's stress.

Then Jake showed me an image of something red and long striking him when he was a puppy. He showed me himself cornered and cowering. Then I heard, "I don't like to be confined!"

Chris had no idea what any of this meant. He said Jake had never been confined.

I asked, "Do you crate him occasionally?"

"No."

"Was Jake ever in a cage?"

"No."

"As a puppy, perhaps?"

"No, never."

Chris said he would never do that to Jake. I didn't know how to ask Chris if he beat his dog, so I asked him if he recalled anything red and long falling or striking Jake as a puppy. Chris said he was unaware of anything striking his dog and suggested that perhaps red was symbolic for the rage he sometimes felt within. However, I knew this was not symbolic. The mental image of a red object his dog delivered was vivid and literal. What was Jake trying to tell me?

After a while, Chris admitted to having beaten Jake with a small, red broom (with the bristles only, he told me) when he was a puppy. He also said that sometimes he threatened Jake with the broom today, but said he was sure that Jake knew he would never hit him again. Wrong. Jake still cringed at the sight of the red broom and the memory of being struck. He had not forgotten the pain. Chris was still using this technique as a threat to gain power and control over his dog. After our discussion, Chris promised never to raise the broom to Jake again.

Although I had covered many issues with Jake, I felt I hadn't really nailed the problem. Yet I could not pull any more information out of the dog or Chris. As we were ending the session, Chris and I talked about his life and what he did for a living. Chris told me that he had traveled around the world. He loved traveling and was planning to leave for another month.

"Oh," I said, "what do you do with Jake when you travel?"

Chris said he brought Jake to the kennel.

"Where Jake is confined in a cage?"

Chris was dumbfounded. A cage had never entered his mind. Chris had no idea how much Jake dreaded being confined, but this was the crux of Jake's anxiety. Jake never knew where Chris was taking him when he jumped into the car.

This is a classic example of a thought ball. Several images and thoughts flashed simultaneously through Jake's mind, delivering a much larger picture with complex layers that had to be peeled away by asking more questions.

I knew that Chris needed to slow down, spend quality time at home, shut off the car radio, and be present with Jake. Above all, he needed to be honest and tell Jake where they were headed in the car. I asked him to inform his dog before he traveled and tell him how long he would be gone. Most importantly, I told Chris he needed to be sensitive to Jake's feelings. He needed to either get a house sitter when he traveled or to stop traveling. It was not fair to Jake to confine him in a cage. I don't know what happened between Chris and Jake. I never heard from him again.

Joey's Deadline

My friend, Loren, called me from Canada to ask for help with her neighbor Rene's Corgi mix. Darlene had given up on the dog and had scheduled an appointment to euthanize him Joey's eyes would glaze over, Loren said, and he would sometimes attack. Sometimes he would sneak up and growl at Rene in her bed. Rene had seen several vets, trainers, and behaviorists, but Joey had not improved.

I offered my services free of charge for Joey's sake—but I was unwilling to do a third-party session. I needed to talk directly to Rene to establish an energy connection. I also needed to know that everyone was open to my doing the communication with Joey. If Rene was skeptical or not invested, she might block the communication flow, which would influence the reading and cause fruitless results.

Rene never contacted me. Loren informed me that Joey was a different dog when he was in her company. When his eyes glazed over, Loren told him to come back in a firm, low, calm voice. It worked. Since Loren was a friend, I went ahead and took a look at Joey's chakras. I found the same energy centers that were either off balance or shut down in Joey were also off balance or shut down in Rene. I ruled out physical problems and entity attachment (misplaced, lost spirits that vibrate at low levels of negativity and attach to or inhabit a human or animal's body when that body is also vibrating at low frequencies). Although Joey was a rescue, I ruled out behavioral issues related to former owners. Even if Joey had experienced some past trauma that surfaced occasionally, his behavior was exacerbated in the presence of Rene. I knew he was reflecting her in some way. I needed to speak to her.

Excited about these findings, I called Loren. When I described what was going on with Joey, Loren said it sounded just like Rene.

She felt overwhelmed and victimized and fell apart at the blink of an eye. She did not know how to take the upper hand in her life or in Joey's. Loren said Rene's eyes often glazed over. Joey held an honest portrait of his person. Had Rene taken a look at herself? I was confident that I could make headway with Joey, but I never got the chance. Rene had Joey destroyed that morning.

There are many stories like this. Sometimes the gap extends too wide and all hope is buried alive in the chasm between human and animal. When an animal's viewpoints are heard and feelings and emotions are expressed, there is a good chance of resolving issues. Yet animal communicators are often called in last, if at all. Sometimes communicators are expected to resolve a deep-rooted, negative pattern or long-term behavior problem overnight, which is not always possible. As one client told me, "You have two days. Then I'm scheduling an appointment for euthanasia." Would you give yourself two days to recover completely if you were diagnosed with a serious mental or physical disease? Healing and transformation is a process, not an overnight express.

My Crystal Ball

Animal communication is rarely understood. Talk show hosts usually present animal communicators as "pet psychic" entertainment. People think we have magic wands or tricks up our sleeves. Many people doubt animals are capable of having such depth. Communicating with them goes deeper than the mundane level, such as what they like to eat or what they like to do. It also involves connecting to the innate wisdom, or soul of the animal. We are all consciousness expressing itself in different forms.

One person approached me at a fundraising event and asked if she could take my photograph with my crystal ball. If I'd had one, I might have clocked her between the eyes! Someone else once called on the phone and said, "I have my cat on my lap. If you can talk to animals, tell me what he's thinking." Although I could sense that her cat was black, I couldn't read his mind. I don't know what any animal is thinking any more than I know what you are thinking until I sit down and talk to you or engage in dialogue with your animal.

Misconceptions disappear when we realize how animals communicate and we understand how telepathy works and how we use it in our everyday interactions with people. There is no mystery here. Telepathy is our birthright, not a gift. When we drop the skeptic and embrace the psychic within, we all see behind the eyes, hear beyond the ears, and feel with the heart. A "psychic" just feels, sees and hears more deeply, and some of us just practice more.

When I first began communicating with people's animals I worked remotely, from the animal's photograph and in the seclusion of my home, especially because the majority of calls were for missing animals. As a result, I was a bit shy and nervous when in the company of the animal's person. This one time I agreed to visit the home of a client who begged me to do the session in-person. Her indoor cat, who had all four feet declawed, was lost somewhere on the streets. My heart sunk. Half way through the session, I felt something, popped my eyes open and caught her staring at my face. I asked her what in the world she was looking at. Bug-eyed, she asked, "Are you in a trance?" I explained that keeping my eyes shut simply helped me to focus and block out visual distractions. I don't channel information from the Egyptian Gods. I simply communicate to animals. This dear kitty was never found.

I don't refer to myself as a pet psychic. Although I perceive energy as a psychic does, I mostly converse directly with the animals. I am an animal communicator, and I never refer to animals as pets. They are spiritual companions and colleagues. Although "pet" can be an endearing word, it also has condescending connotations.

Throughout the book, I refer to the animal's "person" instead of "owner," because animals are not ours to own. These word choices are important. Words can heighten consciousness, and when consciousness changes, attitudes and shared belief systems change. When animals are viewed for the intelligent beings that they are, humane laws will follow. With that said, your beloved animals will love you anyway, no matter what words you choose or what you do for a living, no matter what you wear or eat, how you smell, how you choose to live your life, or whether or not you have a crystal ball.

CHAPTER 3

YOUR ANIMALS ARE WATCHING— OBSERVE YOUR THOUGHTS

The ocean is a very calm thing, but when the winds
are heavy and high, then it's very choppy.
The wind represents your ego—the higher the ego,
the choppier is a person's life.

Yogi Bhajan, Ph.D.
Master of Kundalini Yoga

I f animals see our thoughts, then why do we have to tell them anything? Shouldn't they just know what we are thinking? Just as we are not tuned in to one another unless we choose to listen, our animals are not tuned into us around the clock. Our minds process a thousand thoughts per minute; our thoughts are all over the place and not focused in present time. When our animal companions do choose to tune in to our human minds, all they might hear is static.

How present are we? In Buddhist meditation, mindfulness is practiced during every activity. My Zen teacher would advise: when eating, just eat. Be aware of taste, texture, flavors, chewing, swallowing. When walking, pay attention to sounds around you, the thoughts inside you, smells, internal sensations in the body and external sensations, like your feet contacting the ground. Paying attention reshapes our perceptions.

Paying attention to my discomfort in Zazen (formal Zen sitting meditation with legs folded in the traditional lotus posture and feet on opposite thighs) presented a choice. Either resist, squirm, change position until another irritation arose somewhere else in my body and mind, or focus on my breath and pay attention to the feelings present in my legs, and to the thoughts about those feelings. Noticing our tendency to avoid anything uncomfortable. I noticed that my pain was not constant but was a series of changing sensations that rose and then faded away. Sometimes my legs tingled, throbbed, or burned, and sometimes the pain disappeared completely. This is the nature of reality. Nothing is permanent. What we resist, persists.

When we believe our thoughts or emotions are permanent states and either cling to or resist them, we create suffering for ourselves. We can let our thoughts and emotions toss us around or we can ride them like a surfer riding waves on an ocean. Our thoughts and tumultuous emotions, like the waves themselves, will pass. Our mind, like the ocean, remains untouched. When we stay mindful of what arises within us and allow the experience and feeling of an angry emotion to run through us without reacting, repressing, or mulling it over forever, we are no longer affected by the emotion or any other random wave. Our minds soften instead of harden into a wall of pain. So no matter what hits us, our hearts stay open. We don't shut ourselves down in isolation, become desensitized to other's pain, or drown in our own. When we stay open with our pain our compassion naturally deepens, and we have have the ability to feel the pain of others.

Our animals are content and balanced when we arrive with "surfer mind"—a mind that rides the waves. A mind that is flexible and happy, like their own! Living with animals becomes a heart-centered practice and a life long process of growing our compassion.

For the most part, animals live with each changing moment, accept what arises, and allow things to pass. They are Zen masters. Perhaps this is why my cats did not mind the pounding bass from the street music below or the continuous, high-pitched hum of the neighbor's air conditioner upstairs. The cats napped below the noisy box in apparent bliss. Our resistance creates hell.

So when a fly buzzed around my head during another sitting meditation session, I chose to drop the mental fight, the desire for comfort and the impulse to shoo it away. I focused on my breathing as the insect grazed around my ear canal. I sat perfectly still, present with tickles and buzzing, and I dropped the fearful thoughts of the fly entering my ears or nostrils. I sat until the annoyance turned into the most melodious, soothing sound bath that I had ever heard. As soon as I let go of my resistance and merged with the insect's joyful language, it flew away.

Animal Wisdom 101

I noticed my cats sniffing the air one day. It appeared that they were smelling layers of scents. Their noses twitched, and their heads rose up and down so subtly one would have to stare as intently as I did to notice the nuances of their body movements.

I tried it! Gliding my head up and down, side to side, I became aware of sweet and pungent plant fragrances, sour smog smell, notes of exhaust fumes, and damp wood. Next, down on my hands and knees, I smelled grass the way my cats smelled grass, with my nostrils brushing each blade. I hoped my neighbors hadn't seen me crawling in the yard. I could almost taste the candied smell spanning the musty dirt while the feathery strands tickled my nose, which I buried in the cool green carpet. Wow. Life is vibrant when we pay attention.

Just as I had distinguished the layers of sensations dancing through my sleeping legs in Zazen, I also found that sound and taste were also not just solid blankets of sensation. Now my cats had taught me that smell was no different. It too had a flow of complex layers. We can learn to sense those layers of sounds and smells above us, below us and around us, and learn to heighten our awareness of our surroundings, as if we were savoring all the notes and fragrances of an aged sauvignon. When we walk around drunk in thought, we miss the subtle sips of life.

In addition to showing us how to love unconditionally, animals want us to be present. Yet during most of our waking hours, we operate on automatic and are not at all aware that we are even thinking! What messages are we sending out to our animals? The more aware we are of ourselves, the more aware we are of the impact our unconscious thoughts have on our animals. Here are some stories about what animals do when we are in robot mode.

Seeing A Fight

Nan joked that her house was a "kitty vortex" after she inherited Charlie, her sixth cat. She said this animal dropped from the sky. At the time her cat, Tara, was ill and aging. Nan did not want any more cats. And then Charlie showed up dirty, starving, and limping. Nan simply offered downtrodden Charlie her home.

Oh no. Pure white Charlie was a survivor, and he was determined to hunker down. Snow, Nan's other solid white male, did not intend to let that happen. The two white boys fought viciously—fur flying, and cats screeching and rolling as one, as if they were in a cartoon. Every day Nan returned from work to find fur clumps everywhere and bloody scrapes on the boys.

Certainly, these cats had their reasons to fight. Charlie didn't like the way Snow smelled.

"His mouth stinks!" Charlie said. (Snow had serious teeth and gum issues.) After our first communication session, the boys tolerated each other, but occasionally a fight would ensue when both cats were with their humans in the same room. I told Nan not to think about them fighting, because if she did, that would be the mental message she would be sending them: to fight. However, this is like telling someone not to think of pink elephants.

Then Nan made a remarkable discovery. She noticed that when she was relaxed and forgot about the cats, they got along. When she anticipated a fight out of fear, worry, or anxiety, they did exactly what she dreaded. Nan realized she had to make a conscious effort to think happy, positive thoughts while in their company. As she did, the boys soon responded, curling up together to take a nap on the same bed. Nan relaxed. Charlie and Snow never fought again.

Please Don't Take Me Back!

Bernie the Beagle was intentionally peeing on the rug just off to the side of the pee pad that his guardian, Don, had put out for his dog to use. Bernie knew darned well where to aim.

The first thing I heard when I tuned into Bernie was, "I don't want to go back." I heard this repeatedly, accompanied by feelings of extreme sadness and also an image of a small white dog. Bernie had low self-esteem and did not feel worthy. But why? Who was taking him back, and to where? And who was the white dog?

When I asked these questions, Don burst into tears. His companion, Belle—a small white terrier who had lived with Don for fourteen years—had passed away three months ago, just prior to Bernie's arrival. Don's grief was a pile of bricks. He could not help but think of Belle every time he looked at Bernie. He felt even worse as he admitted to me that he got angry with his new Beagle and often threatened to "take him back."

Don said Bernie had come from a rescue that had already placed him with four different families, each of whom had ended up taking him back to the rescue. I realized that Bernie peed out of insecurity, fear, and dread of being sent back to the rescue for the fifth time.

I told Bernie that Don did not mean what he said, and that he had a forever home with Don. He would not be replaced or compared to Belle, but would be loved for who he was. After that, Bernie used his pad. Don did his part by watching his thoughts. Once he understood the impact his grieving had on Bernie, he poured his attention on his Beagle and stopped focusing on the past.

Stay Away! A Tale of Aggression

Pierre was a Pit Bull from Beverly Hills who lunged at people and at other dogs who passed by. Because he had bitten someone once, his guardian, Simona, was afraid to walk him. She feared getting sued—or worse yet, having her dog taken away and euthanized—if Pierre bit someone again.

When I asked Pierre what was up, I received no reply. Pierre seemed to not consciously know why he did this. He just knew it was the right thing to do as he picked up Simona's fears.

"You must not think about Pierre biting anyone. He sees this image in your mind," I told her. "Try to relax. Trust him more."

Simona, an introvert, unknowingly kept others at bay. The traffic stressed her, and she no longer liked living in Los Angeles. Was Pierre keeping her path clear by keeping people and dogs away? Simona wasn't convinced that she had anything to do with this until the day she walked Pierre with a friend. The two women talked and laughed. As Simona genuinely enjoyed her walk with her friend, she loosened her grip on the leash, forgetting about her dog. She didn't even notice who passed.

After an hour, it hit her. Pierre had been walking by many people and plenty of dogs, but he had not once lunged, growled, or lashed out at anyone. Eventually, Simona sold her Beverly Hills condo and moved to rural Arizona. Pierre, now as relaxed as Simona, continued to be a happy, friendly, and people-loving dog.

Just Doing My Job

Personalities clash sometimes, even when we're best friends. Tinker was a needy but loyal Yorkshire Terrier who snapped at his mate, Merlin. Merlin was a confident, well-balanced, easy-going white West Highland Terrier with many friends. Merlin tolerated Tinker and told me, "I'm the only friend he has." It was true! Tinker was a persnickety old man who preferred sitting in the house with his people than romping outdoors at the park with other dogs.

Tinker had not one single friend except for Merlin, whom he adored. So why did Tinker sometimes snap at him? When I asked Tinker this question, he showed me an image of his person, Selena. Was Selena snapping at her husband, I wondered? It turned out that Selena snapped at Merlin when he jumped on people. She wanted this behavior to stop, but never dreamed that her dog Tinker would take it upon himself and step in to help her.

Be mindful of your thoughts. Your animals will step in and show you any unfinished business and will demonstrate to you that which you need to see or do. They aim to please you, and they'll do their best to act out what they perceive in your mind.

Bubby had pleaded with me to not argue with my partner, and Baba Looie licked my tears when my world toppled down. Ku Ku knocked my face when my mind stuck to unthinkable memories. Anu bit my chin when my attention wandered away from petting him; he always knew when I went into robot mode and reminded me to be here now, present and awake.

My cat O'Henry—named after the chocolate peanut bar, not the author—always knew when I had a heavy heart and would lie across my chest. Having a dose of him in bed every morning was more mind-altering than any therapy I knew of. The power of purr, vibrating at 5,000 beats per second, has got to burn right through our high-functioning brains. O'Henry used his whole body to keep me on track.

Pay Attention!

I scurried through the rooms, multi-tasking as usual and thinking of three thousand things at once. Relaxed? Hardly! O'Henry side-stepped me, thrust himself before my feet, threw me the laser look, and peed right there on the rug. This is shock therapy at its best. Immediately, I got it. Slow down! I thanked O'Henry, surprising him with a grin, and told him I would be more conscious now and forever after. O'Henry never did that again.

Mindfulness is the practice of aliveness. Presence is the spirit in which our animals experience life. When we are present we feel connected to everything around us. Although we have peeks of this awareness, we mostly pull inward and feel separate instead of integrated in the whole. We perceive the world from our self-centeredness. But animals receive the world in its wild magnificence and blossom into each day. They live in the moment. They don't pack their days with negative residues from yesterday or anxieties about tomorrow. We cannot hold on to the present moment, but we can notice our thoughts, let them pass like clouds in the sky, and experience our illusive and eternal nature—the peace and joy, the spirit and momentum in our lives. And we can experience the still spot within, where our animals reside. Mindfulness may be a crawl in the grass toward enlightenment.

BLESSING 1

Quieting The Mind

This audio (.mp3) meditation recording will guide you through an awareness technique that will help to slow the chatter in your mind while you become aware of your thoughts. With practice, your mind will become still and your senses more acute. Eventually, you will be able to hear your own thoughts and decide whether you want to run with them or remain present with your breathing. This meditation will keep your mind alert and show you a method of breathing that will keep you out of robot mode and help you to hear your animals more clearly. A .pdf file demonstrating meditation postures is included.

BLESSING 2

Meditation To Increase Intuition

This Kundalini Yoga Breath Meditation is demonstrated on video. The breathing exercise stimulates the pineal and pituitary glands and increases your intuition. A .pdf file, listing foods that are beneficial for developing these intuitive centers in the brain, is included.

Read more about both of these Blessings at the end of the book.

CHAPTER 4

YOUR UNRESOLVED EMOTIONS—
AND YOUR ANIMAL'S BEHAVIOR

We can no longer view ourselves as isolated
from our environment, and our thoughts as the private,
self-contained workings of an individual brain.
Every thought we have, every judgment
we hold—however unconscious—is having an effect.

Lynne McTaggart
The Intention Experiment

S ome of us hold back from speaking our truth and expressing our thoughts, not facing our fears, not forgiving ourselves or loving ourselves like we ought to. Some of us work jobs we hate, and some of us are not fulfilling our dreams. We hide our anger, intolerance, and pain as we put on a smile. Or maybe we don't smile and we look as miserable as we feel.

We may be stuck and unable to move forward. We may not believe in ourselves, as our animals wholeheartedly do, or feel ourselves worthy in the glorious way that our animals regard us. Perhaps we don't have the respect and admiration from others that we feel we deserve. We may ignore the most important things in life, those things that could enrich our lives, feed our souls, and create everlasting internal happiness and bliss—simply loving what is and who we are.

Wait! I think I may have said this before. You can fool others, and you can fool yourself, but you cannot fool your all-seeing companions. Your animals are your mirrors, and they are talking to you. Are you listening?

I'll Show Them!

Zelda, a black Doberman mix, was aggressive while on the leash. She barked at people and dogs and showed her teeth when she was with her person, Penelope. Twice, Zelda bit a friend's dog when the dog was playing with Penelope's cat. I knew Zelda felt she needed to protect her family—but why? I wasn't surprised to find that Zelda's heart and root chakras were off balance. These same energy centers were off in Penelope. When the heart chakra (fourth chakra) is off balance, one feels abandoned, undeserving, or sad. The root chakra (first chakra) relates to our foundation and support. Zelda was mirroring Penelope's unresolved emotions. I asked Zelda to clue me in.

Zelda told me Penelope was fragile and sad. "I don't want anyone to mess with her. It's too much to bear. All this suffering. She does not know herself, and her mind wanders. She is not focused or ready. She is led by the wind. She blames herself for everything. She is overwhelmed and feels attacked. I am showing her how to fight and not be stepped on. She feels small. She cries. She's hurt."

Zelda sure had a lot to say. I told Zelda she needed to allow Penelope to address her own problems, and that it would make Penelope happy if Zelda relaxed and stopped biting other animals.

Penelope said Zelda was a changed dog after the session. "She listens," Penelope said, "seems so much happier and plays with other dogs, including the one she had a problem with." Sometimes, just getting things out to the surface is enough to resolve these issues. One year later, I contacted Penelope. Since then, she had made many changes in her life—thanks to her dog Zelda.

Fight Back!

I had a similar case with two fighting feline boys. Fernando surprise-attacked Edward when he was sleeping or eating. He told me his person, Janet, did not have the support she needed.

"She doesn't fight back." No wonder Fernando chose to cannonball his roommate, Edward, when Edward was in a vulnerable, no-fight mind zone.

What I love about animals is that they are clear and direct. This is how I know I am hearing their voice and not my own. Although their thoughts come through in my own voice, as if they were my own thoughts, the delivery is spontaneous and simmers with the animal's personality, attitude and inflection. Without a doubt, their voices are unmistakable and unique, and what they share with me is always a surprise.

She's A Pain In The Ass

A woman approached me with her rescued foster dog, Dino. I volunteered my services that day for a Los Angeles-based rescue and dog adoption organization that hosts an annual fundraising marathon. The woman said she wanted to keep Dino, but not if the feisty Chihuahua continued to bite and nip the woman's sister, who lived in the same house. If this behavior continued, Dino would have to move on.

When I asked Dino why he bit the sister this is what he told me: "She doesn't do any work in the house. She's lazy and a pain in the ass."

The woman turned scarlet. She confirmed that her sister never lifted a finger in the house, didn't have a job and was a sort of couch potato.

What? Does an animal care what we do? Do they judge us? Does it matter if we have a high-powered job or sit in front of the TV eating chocolates? Weren't animals in our lives to show us unconditional love, accepting and loving us no matter who we are and forgiving us no matter what we do?

Animals do love us unconditionally. It was the woman who was bugged by her sister's behavior. It was she who held her feelings back and avoided confrontation. So Dino stepped forward and spoke the woman's mind.

Sadly, I was only doing quick fifteen minute sessions that day at the event, and the woman left before I had connected the dots. I hope she eventually made the connection herself and found the courage to come forth with her unresolved feelings. Otherwise, dear Dino, who was merely helping the woman he loved, would be tossed back into the rescue organization until he found another foster mom.

By the way, animals don't swear. I do. It's all in the interpretation.

Go Back to Work For Crying Sake!

Both Lavender and Amelia were indoor kitties urinating on the carpets. I talked first to Amelia, the sixteen-year-old. Amelia had issues with her person, Terry. "Terry doesn't have to be so frantic. It makes me nervous. She's overloaded. I've known her for a long time. I'm not new here. She was more relaxed before. There is tension in the house, and I don't know what to do. I liked my home before when it was less busy and stressful. Russell (Terry's husband) does not listen to her. I see it all. He feels bogged down. Too much going on."

Terry admitted that her life at home before the birth of her baby had been much more relaxed. She worked then, loved her job and took care of herself. She realized that she had been frustrated that her husband traveled a lot, leaving her alone with their six-month-old baby. Terry was curt and impatient with the cats, she said. She recalled that this was when the soiling began.

Terry made changes in her life by giving herself the TLC she needed. She resumed her yoga practice as before and made a conscious effort to be more loving toward her cats.

I heard from Terry six months later. She said Lavender was more confident now, and both she and Amelia's elimination agenda had changed dramatically, although not completely. They now soiled maybe once every five weeks instead of daily and they were continuing to improve. Terry said she had thought the cats would have appreciated her being home during maternity leave, but the peeing became less frequent when she went back to work. Our animals know what is best for us.

Blessings From Rocko

The lobby of Mary's Chicago apartment building made her six-month-old Pit Bull, Rocko, extremely anxious. He growled at people—especially in the elevator—snapped at passing dogs, and nipped at Mary's other two dogs when Mary walked them together. She was afraid Rocko would bite someone.

Rocko told me he didn't want anyone in his space. "I need to stand up for myself," is what I heard. He felt vulnerable and afraid.

Mary told me Rocko had been left to die in a cage in an abandoned building. His scars indicated that he had been used as a bait dog in dog fighting.

I assumed Rocko had some trauma lingering and that he would benefit from energy healing. I worked with Rocko, and we made some progress, but not a complete turnaround. There was something else going on here, and I missed it. Then I noticed the energy centers unbalanced in Rocko were the same exact centers that were unbalanced in Mary.

I asked Mary if she stood up for herself. Did she speak her mind? "Always!" she replied. "I am direct and up front with all my friends."

Hmmm. I needed to probe a bit here. Mary confided that she didn't leave the house much. She spent every second with Rocko since she was unable to crate train him due to his abandonment issues associated with the cage. She spent entire days with her dogs.

As we continued to talk, Mary suddenly burst into tears. Her husband was away on business trips more frequently now, she said, and she hated it when he left. She fell apart and felt vulnerable and afraid. But Mary had not told this to her husband. She knew her husband had no other option, and she did not want to create more stress in his life, so she tucked all her feelings inside.

Rocko was "speaking up" for Mary by not allowing anyone near her space. Mary agreed to go out more with her friends and communicate openly with her husband, which she finally did. I spoke to her one year later. She said she realized that, in her husband's absence, Rocko had become the little man around the house, protecting her. It had surprised her that Rocko could intuit so much about her in a few short months. However, it is not by accident or coincidence that we attract specific animals into our lives who will help us triumph difficult times. The short chunk of time they are with us does not affect the job they are brought here to do. No doubt Mary and Rocko probably shook hands and signed a pact before either of them took birth.

Rocko was still sometimes triggered by things Mary said, but now she was more confident and swiftly redirected him to a calm state. Rocko grew more affectionate and smiled all the time now, she said, squinting his eyes and curling his upper lip to give the biggest toothy grin!

Own Up!

Timmy was one of seven cats. He often attacked one of the other cats, Sumi, pinning her down and hurting her. He ran from his person, Laura, when she passed by or even looked at him. Laura called, expecting me to fix things up. After all, I claim to be an animal communicator.

Timmy had been showing aggressive behavior for two years. I was the cat's last chance. Great. I did my best but was not successful. Timmy said Laura did not like him. He showed me Laura's roommates fighting and shutting him out of their room when Laura was gone.

Laura said she loved all her cats but did not like Timmy's behavior and was thinking of finding another home for him. These cases are difficult. Animals know when you are thinking of giving them up, and this can create anxiety for the animal and exacerbate the problem. This problem had many layers, I knew, and I could feel resistance from Laura. Yet I was expected to turn Timmy around overnight.

I had a heart-to-heart talk with Timmy. He was mad. He told me Laura was not taking responsibility. She needed to speak out. She was not being up front with herself or her boyfriend. Her needs were not met. "There's chaos below the surface. Can you feel it? I can!

Laura does not want to be here. She's not 100 percent! Laura needs to own up!"

I had no idea what this meant, or that Laura even had a boyfriend. Indeed, Laura's boyfriend lived in Santa Cruz, and Laura spent six months at a time there and six months in San Diego, grounded in neither place. It was about two years earlier that Timmy had started acting out—the same time that Laura had started pulling away emotionally from her life at home. She didn't want to be here and was planning a permanent move to Santa Cruz in the future. Meanwhile, when she was gone, Timmy was left with the quarreling couple. Animals do not like us attacking one another.

Timmy's behavior improved at first, but then I did not hear back from Laura until I contacted her months later. She said Timmy's behavior had not changed. He was still beating up Sumi, and she still had to separate them. Thankfully, she did not get rid of him. Interestingly enough, she didn't remember any of what Timmy had said about her. Had she made any commitments either way regarding her living situation? I don't know. The roommates were still there. Were they getting along? Timmy's aggression continues, and he still runs from Laura, not willing to face her until Laura faces herself. Sometimes I wish I had a magic wand.

Separation Anxiety Teacher

Carol's purebred Afghan Hound, Dali, came to her unsocialized and wild at ten months old. Dali tore the house up whenever he was left alone, even for two hours. Carol said it looked as though Edward Scissorhands had been there when she returned. She found stuffing from the new living room cushions everywhere. Dali discovered her suitcase and pulled out a bag of stuff. He went into the bathroom and chewed the lids off cleaning products. He also chewed her duvet, rugs, and plants. He even found his way to her closet to chew her favorite shoes. She had tried crating him only to return to an overturned water bowl, urine sprayed all over the walls, and the crate door broken off its hinges.

Carol was afraid to leave the house, anticipating the remains of a tornado when she returned. I had a talk with Dali.

Dali told me Carol took on way too much and did not listen. She wasn't taking care of herself. Dali wanted to see Carol truly enjoying herself with friends at the house. He also did not feel that he met Carol's expectations. There was much fear involved and a feeling of panic and being trapped. I knew this went beyond Dali not wanting to be left alone. Both he and Carol had the same chakras off balance in their bodies.

Nothing seemed to change much after the sessions, so I did several rounds of EFT, the Emotional Freedom Technique that I used for Mickey. I did this remotely, using myself as a surrogate and tapping for Carol as well.

Carol reported immediate improvement. She said she left the house in one-hour increments, gradually increasing to a full day. Then Carol took a long look at herself and embarked on an inner journey of healing. Using neurofeedback, Carol had a brain scan which showed she suffered from post-traumatic stress disorder, which led to low self-esteem. "Freezing," in Carol's words, "and all those fun, fear-based challenges." Carol realized that she had been lost in grief over the death of her elderly Pit Bull, Isabelle, as well as over the ending of an intense long-term relationship. Carol had filed bankruptcy shortly before all this happened, and found herself in a frenzy afterwards—still grieving, alone and broke—when she had to find another place to live.

Once Carol understood what caused her constant anxiety, she learned skills to cope with her addictive personality. Carol became proactive instead of freezing when confronted with challenges. She made more time for her social life, and she learned to let things roll off her back rather than ruminating on the situation, imagining what terrible thing might happen next.

Once Carol had her anxiety under control, she found that Dali let his anxiety roll off his back. When she left, Dali never destroyed the house again. He grew to be an amazing tall, slender show dog who won many competitions.

She's Ruining My Life

Would I be able to save Mimi's life? Trainers and behaviorists could not stop this Pit Bull from chewing the furniture whenever her person, Charles, left. Mimi had gnawed the table legs to a pulp and destroyed the outdoor front gate three times in a desperate panic attack to get out and sit in the neighbor's yard. Mimi had been doing this for years. Every time Charles repaired the damage, she destroyed the same spot the next day.

Charles had scheduled an appointment for Mimi's euthanasia when his friend called me begging for help. He postponed the appointment and allowed a window of time for me to work with Mimi. I felt the pressure and skepticism from Charles. He had given up.

When I walked into the house, I was greeted by an affectionate, sweet dog. Mimi had much to share. She knew she was not pleasing her person and that she made Charles unhappy. She felt that she had failed at her job, and there were too many loose ends to tie up. She said Charles was filled with extreme sadness. "He won't listen. He has to do everything his way. He's a nonstop man. He needs to slow down and focus, too. He is not there inside. He is everywhere. I am grounding for him. I give him something solid to hold onto, but sometimes I fail—like when I chew things up." Charles attended recovery programs and, like Mimi, had a history of addictive behaviors.

Mimi said her head swirled sometimes. Chewing kept her focused. Most of Mimi's chakras were off balance, and her throat chakra was completely shut down. Mimi was not being heard and she needed a creative expression. Although Charles took her to work with him most of the time, she was bored whenever left behind and didn't like the dark house. The blinds were kept shut. The sound of the vacuum cleaner also frightened Mimi—but after a few rounds of EFT, Mimi, although shaking, stood with me by the noisy machine as it swept across the floor.

After a few minutes of healing energy, Mimi sighed and sank into a blissful dream state. When Charles left the house the next time, Mimi did not even follow him to the door as she usually did. When he returned, nothing had been destroyed. Mimi continued to improve, but she had relapses that disheartened Charles. She needed work, and I needed time, but the hourglass was almost empty.

Then one day, there was a miraculous, although oddly sudden, change in Charles. He greeted me at the door with calm confidence and told me he had gotten a handle on his life and had finally taken the alpha role with Mimi. Focused and optimistic, he admitted that Mimi had been a spoiled princess and that things were different now. Euthanasia, he said, was out of the question.

I had been working with Mimi free of charge for the short time that Charles allotted. Since he didn't ask me to continue working with Mimi, and since I was falling in love with her, I stepped back to give

51

them both some space and readjustment time. Was Charles willing to look at himself, and at his relationship with his dog, and make the changes in himself that would provide Mimi with the stability she needed? Months went by, and I never heard from Charles. He never replied to my phone calls or e-mails. I tried contacting him through his friend, who originally called me for help, but got no reply. I feared the worst, but I chose to imagine both Charles and Mimi living so well that no one had a need to contact me. Months later, I learned that Mimi had been euthanized.

The thought that I had failed Mimi was unbearable. Yet to keep balance and confidence in the work I do, I had to remember soul contracts. Charles and Mimi had their karma to work through and their lessons to learn in this lifetime. We can only do our best to help, guide, and support each other. We can never force anyone to come around if they are not ready, if it is not time, or if it is not for their highest benefit. We all need space to grow and time to heal. Yet, with that said, I still cannot help but wonder if there was something I missed or something more I could have done for Mimi. May she rest in peace.

CHAPTER 5

THE DOG GONE TRUTH—
ANIMALS ARE EMPATHS

We are certainly not the only beings
motivated by feelings of compassion
and concern for others. Altruism is
widespread in the animal kingdom.

Gary Kowalski,
The Souls of Animals

I was always told I was too sensitive and that my compassion was out of balance. I never understood why I felt agitated and exhausted in crowds and under bright lights, such as those found in shopping malls or Las Vegas. An empath absorbs the feelings, emotions and energy of others like a sponge and can become overwhelmed.

Our animals feel our true emotions, those we keep hidden from the surface. We can fool the world and even ourselves, but we cannot fool our animal companions. Animals are highly sensitive empaths.

The Barker

Kelly wanted to know why her Chihuahua, Gia, barked ferociously and nonstop at her roommate, Sam, when he walked through the door. Sam was no stranger to Gia, and liked the little dog. When I tuned into Gia, I felt extreme anxiety and concern. I interpreted Gia's thoughts this way: "Sam is tight! He's so tight and all over the room!" Sam's energy caused Gia to feel excited and scattered, and she mirrored this feeling back to Sam. Kelly agreed that Sam entered the house like a storm, often tense and agitated from work and the heavy commute in traffic. Now Sam's tension infused Gia's barking, and the nerve-racking cries overwhelmed the rooms, which didn't help Sam, who was already stressed.

Bhola The Garbage Eater

Bhola was a Border Terrier who ate garbage from the bathroom. Could this have been the only room in the house where the energy was grounded and neutral, because it was where the family took care of themselves? Bhola told me he wanted his people to release and let go. He wanted his person Denise to focus. She "took on too much in the house." She had little time for herself, and she needed to open her heart and love herself. Bhola told me Denise's husband, Ajeet, needed to "relax and let happen." Ajeet's fear did not allow him to trust life, Bhola said, and he held on too tightly.

Denise told me Ajeet expected perfect obedience from Bhola, especially on the leash. Bhola ran away every chance he got. Bhola told me he liked to run and had to curb his ways for his humans. Coming from an Eastern Indian culture, Ajeet did not allow Bhola in the bedroom or the upstairs hallway leading to the bedrooms. Bhola felt left out. The bathroom was a shared family room. Eating garbage soothed his anxiety, got the attention of his people, and helped with the scattered and constricted energy he felt throughout the house. Bhola had found a way to restore the balance.

I Don't Know Why I'm So Sad

Maiko came to me in tears. Tiny, her elderly Yorkie, no longer wanted to play in the park with the other dogs. Tiny had arthritis, and Maiko feared it was progressing. At the park, Tiny just sat by Maiko the entire time. Maiko believed her dog was in severe pain and that his painful condition now compromised his quality of life. She could not stop crying. With Tiny's permission, I mentally entered his body through the crown chakra, located at the top of the head, to see if I could feel the severity of pain and where it was located. I felt nothing.

Was he on medication, I asked? He was, and apparently it was working. I then asked Tiny why he wasn't playing in the park. I received no response, only extreme sadness. I realized this was not Tiny's problem. I turned to Maiko. There was nothing wrong with Tiny, I reassured Maiko, and I told her that she needed to lighten up! She had to stop crying and projecting gloom and doom into her dog if she wanted him to return to his playful ways. Maiko changed her attitude and called me two weeks later. Tiny was romping in the park again!

I'm Popeye the Nurse

Animals know when our energy is blocked and not flowing freely in our bodies, so they know when we are sick. They know where we hurt and can smell disease. Empaths are natural born healers.

My neighbor Popeye, a tea cup Chihuahua, no longer wanted to go for walks with me. She barked when I came to the door and tossed her head back toward the bedroom. I took her for short jaunts around the block to get her mind off Michael, her human, who was eighty-three and bedridden. The doctors had found nothing wrong with Michael except that he was severely depressed. Popeye lay next to Michael on the bed day and night and never left his side. Popeye no longer cared about her walks. Nothing was more important than her job as nurse and caring companion.

Giant To The Rescue

I met a young Canadian Veteran, named Johnny, on a retreat. Johnny had been suffering from PTSD, since he returned from combat in Bosnia two years ago. Doctors had put him on fourteen different medications, but Johnny grew more depressed and suicidal. One day he decided to hang himself and took a rope with him into the woods.

Johnny's Rottweiler, a service dog named Giant, had followed Johnny into the woods that day and tugged and pulled on the rope. Johnny was so touched by this altruistic action, he let go of the rope and decided to live.

Giant continues to do amazing things for Johnny. He knows when Johnny is uncomfortable around certain people and will drop his body between Johnny and the person. When Johnny has nightmares, Giant wakes him up. When Johnny says to him, "watch my back," Giant sits back-to-back with Johnny, and when anyone approaches, Giant knocks his head against Johnny's back. Giant is only one-year-old.

I Smell Cancer!

Holly pawed at her person Alisa's left breast every day for two months. When Alisa decided to go for her yearly mammogram, cancer was found in her left breast. After that, Holly knew that Alisa had found help and that her task as messenger was accomplished. She never pawed at Alisa again. Not only had Holly smelled the tumor, she also knew that it didn't belong in Alisa's body. How frustrating it must be when our wisdom is invisible to others. Animals persevere. They understand our limitations and recognize our inability to hear them. They try to get through to us in any way they can.

The Power of Purr

While I was teaching art to children at my home, one six-year-old artist—a pretty blond girl named Mikayla—opened my eyes.

"Baba's dying, Diana" Mikayla said.

"Oh, no honey, he's just not feeling so well. He's going to the vet on Monday."

"No, Diana," she said, "look at him. He's as small as a kitten. He's dying." I had been so preoccupied with my life that I had not even noticed that my fifteen-year-old cat, Baba Looie, had shrunk to half his size. Or perhaps I was blind in denial.

The vet confirmed that Baba did not have much longer to live. Fluid had swelled in Baba's belly, and his heart beat faster than hummingbird wings. I was devastated.

One afternoon, I had a pounding headache. I don't take medication, so I threw myself across the bed and lay there with the pain, waiting to fall asleep. Bubby jumped up and placed his paw on my temple. Then his brother, Baba Looie—who was near death and had been motionless for days in his bed—jumped up and relaxed his body across the back of my head. With both cats forming a circle of healing energy around my head, I brought my attention to my breathing, inhaling and exhaling to the high frequency rhythm of their purrs. Their vibrations penetrated through my head, and within minutes my headache subsided. How compassionate and altruistic our companions are, even when they are nearing their own transition.

Children also are naturally in tune with their feelings and emotions. Their intuition is fresh and unhindered, having not yet been discounted and diminished. With as little as twenty minutes of training, my young six to ten-year-old students learned to send and receive thoughts with animals. They didn't doubt themselves or have expectations. They approached animal communication with eager excitement, as though they were diving into another experimental painting project. We sat in our sacred, sharing circle on the floor and took turns.

One eight-year-old boy told my assistant, Joy, that her dog, Spooky, loved to walk in the park. The boy described a bench under a tree and a circular cement walkway running through the park. He said he smelled pizza. The class burst out laughing. Joy confirmed the boy's findings and told us that her dog's favorite activity was going to the park. Joy, her son, and Spooky often walked along the cement pathway and sat on a bench under the tree while Spooky played. On the way to and from the park, they passed an Italian restaurant!

How receptive, insightful, and empathic children are. Keeping their hearts open, listening, and staying in present moment awareness most of the time, they make good candidates for animal communicators.

Plants Are People Too

Plants not only have emotions and empathy, but they can also sense our intentions, just as any other living being can. One day while watering his plants, Cleve Backster decided to hook up a polygraph machine to one plant to measure how long it took for the water to rise up the stem. Backster, who founded the Backster School of Lie Detection, was the leading lie detector expert in the country. The Lie Detection machine reacts to our nervous system and shows a response that corresponds to whether we are excited or relaxed.

Backster was shocked to discover that the plant showed alarm when he had dumped boiling hot water down the drain that scorched invisible bacteria. The plant reacted the same way when he held a burning match under its leaves. However, more surprisingly, the plants did not react when they understood that Backster was bluffing. Plants could feel our intentions.

Trees warn one another telepathically when they realize they are about to be massacred. One day I returned home to find the gardeners "cutting back" the yard. They were told to trim the big Chinese elm, which had taken years to drape itself to the ground and provided a thick fence of privacy from the noisy street below. Now the yard looked like a war zone with young men positioned throughout the massive branches hacking the main arteries of the tree. Their thick, masculine arms were amputated to short stumps. The workers destroyed the trellice of bluebells that canopied the garden steps, and continued to destroy everything else that had grown full and plump, until the yard was empty and bare. I could now see all the houses on the street below and clear into the neighbor's yards on either side. The remaining shade plants would be scorched by the sun. The skimpy, elm branches that survived dangled timidly with no purpose or design. It looked as if a bomb had hit. Feeling powerless, I consoled myself with thoughts about them growing back someday, and believed what others had thought of me; I was "too sensitive."

At three o'clock in the morning I was awakened by a long, high-pitched humming noise. I sat up in bed with a wrench inside my gut. The sound welled inside my body, and tears rolled from my eyes. I opened the bedroom window to hear where this whine was coming from. To my surprise, it permeated the entire back space. It was coming from the elm. The tree was in extreme distress, and it was screaming.

Just then my cat, O'Henry, laid across my chest and purred into my heart center. I cried to him. I told him it was time to move, that we could no longer stay here and continue to live in this open, barren, death-ridden space. How could I bear to look at the elm's deformed body? Her majestic arms chopped off at her trunk? Suddenly O'Henry's thoughts cut right through my sadness. "Life isn't about trees," he said. "It's about growing. You are growing. I am growing. The trees are growing. Everything is fine."

My Zen teacher had once said something similar; "Everything is perfect as it is. Everything is a process evolving." A profound truth, embedded in the fabric of Taoism and Zen. A realization and acceptance of the way things are. An underlying awareness of the fundamental condition of life on earth; pain was inevitable. This didn't mean we sat back and watched others suffer. We always step in to help, take action and propagate seeds for change. But we didn't have to suffer in the process. Resistance created our suffering; our mind created both our mental and physical pain. If we stayed open through our pain, and through the pain of others, we can develop our compassion.

Wasn't this what we humans were here to learn? Developing compassion and loving ourselves and others was essential for our growth and evolvement. Our animals were here to help us with this. They feel our pain and stay with us through our healing process.

CHAPTER 6

DIS-EASE, YOUR ANIMALS—AND YOUR REPRESSED EMOTIONS

*Perhaps we can say we are only alive when we
live the life of the world, and so live the joys
and sufferings of others.*

Thich Nhat Hanh
The Miracle of Mindfulness

Negative emotions and stress can change the harmonious pattern of your DNA and weaken your immune system, creating an opportunity for disease to manifest in your body. If animals internalize your negative emotions and repressed desires, it would make sense that illness can manifest in their bodies as a result.

Do animals mirror our physical diseases? I have known animals to develop cancer after their person's cancer went into remission. Penelope and her dog Zelda, both had stomach problems. Penelope later found she had a heart murmur and recently found that Zelda had developed one too. Jane and her cat Abby shared urinary tract infections.

Steve was on heart medication. His sweet brown tabby feline, Mauricio, always draped across his chest. Eventually, Steve's heart condition improved, and he was able to get off the medication—but Mauricio developed heart problems and was now on heart medication himself.

I don't think that Mauricio consciously took on the disease for his beloved person. But I do know that animals are empaths, and I stay open to all possibilities. Animals can feel our emotional wounds and can remain ill until we heal ourselves. The following stories are from my experiences with the animals I have worked with.

Pain Free

Sanda was a German Shepherd who had hip dysplasia, as many of this breed do. Although it would eventually worsen, I witnessed a rapid decline in Sanda's body as her person's severe arthritis rapidly improved. Sanda's person, Jason, noticed the pain in his body lessening. I noticed that Sanda began to have a difficult time walking. Soon, the pain had disappeared from Jason's body. His arthritis was gone. Sanda, however, could no longer get up.

People have asked me to tell their animal not to take on their illness. Where is that crystal ball when I need it? I cannot tell anyone not to get sick. Nothing is that simple. We get sick for many reasons, and many factors influence disease in our body. There are pollutants in the environment, and too many preservatives, chemicals, fat, and sugar in our diet. Fungus and parasites can thrive in our bodies and weaken our immune system.

There is also our karma to consider, experiences we need for spiritual growth and unresolved issues or trauma to be worked out from this life and from past lives. Negative emotions sabotage our well-being. According to Quantum Physics, the biggest factor contributing to our health is our personal set of beliefs about illness. Authors Dr. Bruce Lipton, *The Biology of Belief,* and Dr. Mario Martinez, a clinical neuropsychologist who wrote *The Mind Body Code,* agree that it is one's beliefs that determine whether one will get a particular disease—not the hereditary gene that predisposes you to the disease.

Perhaps disease is part of our soul contracts—an obstacle or blessing manifesting to redirect our lives and present an opportunity for change. In the film *The Living Matrix,* a woman's world fell apart when she developed a particular brain tumor that caused infertility. She had always wanted children, and she wasn't ready to die. After much soul searching and Neuro-Linguistic Programming, she remembered her unhappy childhood and realized that, on a subconscious level, she had not really wanted children.

Her tumor had manifested to protect her from a decision that would not have benefitted her. She noticed that every thought until then had been about attacking and killing the tumor. When she saw this as an inner conflict, she began to acknowledge the blessings, insights and opportunities the tumor had brought her. As she realized how her entire life had changed because of it, she decided to accept the tumor and not treat it as an enemy. She gave the brain tumor permission to stay for as long as it needed to, and the tumor gradually disappeared.

Dr. Bernie Siegel, author of *Love, Medicine & Miracles* and *The Art Of Healing,* among other books, says that self-healing begins with self-love, and that when you send your body messages of love, the message that *you want to live* gets delivered to your immune system. When we love ourselves as our animals love us, we crawl closer toward enlightenment.

I rarely get sick, and when I do I usually turn around in a few days. Yet one time, a case of the flu lingered for several weeks. One evening I sat in a warm tub of water and asked to be shown the emotional cause of the flu. Insights usually surfaced whenever I took a bath. Water is a conductor of energy, and while resting in water, the mind is relaxed and receptive. I soaked and noticed my thoughts.

Suddenly, my cat Anu popped into my mind. His image delivered that all-knowing gut punch I feel when I've hit the truth. I sobbed good and hard. Anu had been killed by a car two weeks earlier, and I had repressed my grief. I cried in the tub, told him I was sorry for not being there for him. As I released my pent up emotions I sent love to him and to every cell in my body.

The flu was gone the next day. Our unconscious thoughts and beliefs play a part in our wellness and sickness. Our animals sometimes bring this to our awareness.

Perfect Timing

Hye Su fell hard when her female brown Labrador, Sienna, tripped her. Darn that dog! Hye Su broke three ribs. After a series of rib and chest x-rays, doctors found cancer on Hye Su's lung. It was still in treatable Stage One, thanks to Sienna for catching it in time. Did Sienna smell the cancer and deliberately trip her person? Since I don't believe in accidents, I believe that, on some level, Sienna did play an integral part in this appropriate timing.

After Hye Su's surgery and during a painful, six-month journey to recovery, Sienna broke a bone in her ankle that would not heal. Sienna did not have cancer, but she had massive complications involving multiple surgeries, casts and treatments, none of which were working.

Vets said amputation was the only option for Sienna, but Hye Su stalked the internet for specialists and alternative treatment for her dog, which in turn took her mind off her own painful concerns and undoubtedly helped Hye Su to heal faster. By the time Hye Su regained her health and strength, Sienna's ankle had healed. Years later, a protuberance on Sienna's left ankle was diagnosed as arthritis. Hye Su also has an arthritic knob on the outside of her left ankle.

Becoming sick is complex. I do my part in my healing practice to channel divine energy and light, unblocking stagnant energy to allow the body to heal itself. The rest is up to you or your animal and God. No one can heal anyone if it is not one's karma to be healed or if one has an unconscious resistance to getting well.

Illness is not a curse. It is the way in which are bodies can communicate to us. Therefore, no one should ever blame themselves or feel guilty if their animal is sick. The picture is always larger than what we see, and again, everything is a process with unexpected blessings. The following stories show ways in which our emotions and thoughts have physically affected the animals close to our hearts.

I'm Crawling Out Of My Skin

I suspected that Garfield had abandonment issues underlying his allergies. I later learned that the cat had known two loving humans in his life. The first was an elderly woman whose children had placed her in a nursing home and left Garfield behind on the city streets to fend for himself. For months, Garfield sat at the door of his home waiting for his human to return and survived the streets for two years. He was a dirty, matted mess and had grown somewhat feral when he met the second woman.

The cat wouldn't allow any human to touch him, but gradually trusted the kindness of this woman, who fed and cared for him at her work place nearby. For five years, Garfield found a Monday through Friday home in the office, where he sat on the woman's lap from nine to five greeting everyone who walked in, until the day the woman changed jobs and left the city. Garfield was left behind on the streets again.

The last thing I wanted was another cat, but Garfield needed a real home, so I took the feisty, orange, homeless, ornery, dominant alpha cat to my home. He bit me and attacked my other male cat O'Henry. But this wasn't the only reason I regretted taking him in. You see, Garfield had an itch.

I spent a small fortune on him, but he would not stop scratching his face and ears to a bloody pulp. Garfield saw pricey dermatologists who did skin scrapings and biopsies. All they could offer were steroids for life. The stray had expensive allergy tests and eight lyme sulphur dips to rule out mites. He saw several allopathic and holistic vets, two homeopaths, and a Chinese chiropractor who muscle tested him for allergies. Garfield tried numerous supplements, antihistamines, vitamins, and herbs. He ate a raw meat diet with no grain, until I realized he was allergic to everything except duck and salmon.

When I found out that another allergen was dust mites, I pulled up the rugs in my one room apartment and bought an air purifier. Garfield slept on magnets and received Rife vibrational sound therapy. I replaced the organic wheat grass litter with green tea litter to rule out possible sensitivity to wheat. Garfield saw two colleague healers. When I tried healing, he bit my hands.

I rubbed his ears daily with coconut oil and put more in his food, and afterwards alternated a variety of supplements such as evening primrose oil, fish oil, aloe vera, turmeric, and colostrum.

Garfield wore Elizabethan collars, but screamed and scratched at the plastic cone. He had a parasite cleanse and was treated for fleas, yeast, and fungus. I put bentonite and montmorillonite clay in his food to detox him of heavy metals and to restore his digestive tract. He ate raw egg yolks and took L-Lysine, kelp and probiotics. Despite my efforts, Garfield's condition got worse.

I finally succumbed and gave him a low dose of steroids, which helped for one year—but the itching slowly crept back again. Garfield continued to scratch intermittently, screaming and shaking his head and splattering blood over the walls, curtains, and floor. He also had three urinary tract blockages during this two year period which required the usual expensive hospitalization. Feeling frustrated, I often wished I had left him on the streets. Then I noticed a pattern.

I worked a physically strenuous, emotionally draining job I did not particularly like due to back stabbing and negativity among the coworkers. The job was not full time, but it came around every two months. A week or two before and during the job, Garfield scratched. I paid more attention to my mood states. It seemed that whenever I was under stress of any kind—even when I was not aware that I was, or when I argued with someone at home or away from my home Garfield scratched until he bled.

It is not so easy to automatically stop a deeply engrained pattern and response to stress. I first needed to become aware of it, and then to keep up a steady meditation and yoga practice to help me stay aware of my negative thoughts, cope with anxiety, and provide a stress-free environment for Garfield. Most of all, I needed to change jobs.

Although stress was not the sole cause of the cat's scratching, it was an obvious contributor. Cats are electrical beings and are especially sensitive to energy. Another contributor was Garfield's history of abandonment, and now here with me, he still didn't have a sure-foot on the ground. He knew I hadn't fully opened my heart to him. I wasn't particularly drawn to him, and I had never wanted to take him in. Now, one year into our relationship, I resented him for the high vet bills I had to pay. Garfield was also an angry cat and a somewhat feral dominant male, who quickly resorted to biting. Between you and me, I didn't like him.

He dropped his anger when I changed my attitude and suddenly fell in love with him. It seemed to happen over night. I realized that this tough, street-cat survivor was really a big baby with a wounded soul, who howled to the heavens if left outside alone for more than thirty minutes. Three years down the road, Garfield rarely scratches, and although he still bites he never breaks the skin.

We're Both Blocked

Perhaps animals do not consciously take on our illnesses. Although it does appear that an animal's ailments will sometimes improve after their people have done the emotional clearing and healing that they needed to do for themselves. In fact, in many cases it is our animal companions who prompt us to take action.

Billy was a black and white tuxedo cat who also had urinary blockages, which are treated by inserting a catheter to flush the crystals out of the urethra. This condition requires intervention within twenty-four hours, or the cat's bladder will burst and a painful death will follow. Often, when people see their cats straining in the litter box, they assume they are constipated, and by the time the cat sees a vet, it's too late.

Helen called me to find out what might be causing the blockages. I connected to Billy and found an extremely timid, sensitive kitty. His lower three chakras, those below the heart center, were completely shut down. As I suspected so were Helen's. Helen had reoccurring problems with her ovaries. Both the bladder and ovaries are second chakra health issues.

Helen needed self-nurturing and much more. Billy told me she was frustrated and unhappy with her job, she felt stuck, and she didn't know how to move forward. I asked Billy what his person did for a living. He told me that Helen worked with people and took home their problems. (Helen worked in an office with negative people that she could not get away from, and she mulled her situation over for hours at home).

I found Helen's energy tense and condensed. She held hurts from her past. No surprise that hard, condensed crystals formed in Billy's bladder. I heard the words "go camping"—but not from Billy. Helen said she had not gone camping in a long time. I felt that connecting with earth energy would be good for her. The three chakras below the heart are related to our foundation, security, vulnerability, self-love, self-esteem, creativity, personal power and our relationship to money.

Helen needed to connect with that grounding, creative energy. As long as she was "blocked," an abundant, peaceful life could not flow to her. I contacted Helen one year later. She was still at the same job, but she had done much inner work and clearing and had found new ways to handle her difficult working situation. She understood that everyone was her teacher. Since Helen began her healing journey, Billy had not had another urinary blockage.

Because motion is within everything in the universe, nothing is at rest. We are vibrational beings. According to the Law of Emergence, the universe always matches our vibrational frequency. In other words, we attract to us, or rather merge with, other living beings and experiences that match the vibrational frequency of our thoughts and emotions. And so it is with our communication with other species. Once we resonate at the same frequency as the animal resonates, we can easily exchange our energetic thought forms, or attract certain animals into our lives who will help us, and even physically approach an animal in the wild and not be perceived by them as a threat. Perhaps vibration and resonance is how two seemingly random events often coincide, which Carl Jung referred to as "synchronicity."

I once gathered in a ceremonial circle with my Shaman teacher in the forest as she disclosed sacred Inca teachings. Hawk circled above us the entire time and flew away when the ceremony was completed. Native Americans have always known wild animals are totems, and their random appearance in our lives may not be so random.

What we put out comes back to us. This is why it is important to know what you are putting out. Our thoughts broadcast out into the universe, and the universe always responds by matching our feeling tone. It is no coincidence that starving, emaciated, homeless dogs often crossed my path during the days when I saw myself as a victim, lost, deeply wounded, and starving in mental pain. External events always match our internal thoughts. Similarly, there may be an analogical connection between our repressed emotions and our animal companion's physical health.

Live Your Dreams

Randy had called me because his dog, Alice, would not go for walks anymore. Alice, a medium built, tan, gentle dog, was concerned about her person, Randy. Alice said he was stuck and unable to move forward. She showed me long periods of silence in the house, with Randy's wife spending countless hours alone in her office, facing the computer. Alice said there was a part of Randy that he was not seeing and allowing to come forth. I had no idea what this might be, so I talked to Randy. He confided that he wanted to take up singing again, but since he had put this desire aside for so long, he was afraid to pursue it. On top of this, his marriage had grown stagnant.

Alice's reason for not walking was due to pain in her hips. Her hind legs occasionally gave out. However, the hips are where we hold fear and indecision that holds us back. The legs carry us forward in life. Lower leg problems relate to fear of the future and not wanting to move ahead.[3]

Express Yourself

Brita also held back her creative expression. She called me from Sweden when her cat, Bo, sprayed in the house. Bo had much to say. One thing Bo shared about Brita was that she liked to ski, and that Brita was bogged down and needed to run more. She was also arguing more with her husband. Bo said he felt Brita's sadness and said she did not stand her ground.

Like most animals who spray, Bo's second and fifth (throat) chakras were off balance. Emotionally, these centers relate to our expansion and verbal or creative expression. When I talked to Brita, she said that she loved to ski and had not gone skiing in a long time. Brita said she used to run every day and missed it. It was something she had been meaning to do again. She agreed that she did not stand her ground. When I viewed Bo's body, I felt stomach indigestion and discomfort. Brita's solar plexus center was off balance. The

---

[3]   You Can Heal Your Life, Louise Hay

solar plexus relates to the stomach. Emotionally, it is our center of confidence, identity and purpose in life.

Our animals sense when our spirits are not soaring. It is as though our animals internalize our incompleteness, and know when our soul is crying for spiritual food. They sense all our repressed feelings. They are our little mandalas, as Jung would have it, bringing us back to wholeness.

CHAPTER 7

HAPPY 'TIL THE END—ANIMALS AND OUR THOUGHTS ABOUT THEIR DEATH

Tell me about the passing of life,
its thin door which is as fragile as life itself...
Lisa Marguerite Mora,
author, editor, friend, Los Angeles

There are some things we don't want to think about. As silly as it sounds, I never thought my animals would die. But eventually, our animals leave us. Some leave tragically, some slowly, some unexpectedly. Some leave home, never to return. Yet no matter how our companions choose to make their exits, when they leave, our lives are changed forever.

The truth is they never really leave us. No one dies. At least this is what I know in my heart, after two of my cats and my mother returned in dreams two months after their passing. These were not ordinary dreams, but ones that touched me in an unforgettable way. If my cat Yudi could relay a message to me in my dream state—a message that saved Baba Looie's life—then why couldn't our departed loved ones get through to us this way, too?

When we sleep, our minds are uncluttered and receptive. We are in the Theta brainwave state and can easily connect and access information from the Unified Field. Theta is a slow wave of brain activity that happens while dreaming, during hypnosis and in the time just before sleeping and waking, which I refer to as twilight sleep, or floating.

In Theta, we are between the conscious and subconscious worlds, where the mind can connect to the Divine and receive information. Remote Viewing[4] is done while the brain is in Theta.

When I dreamed of my departed mother and my beloved cats, the messages were always the same. My mother and both cats had each come to say goodbye, to say they were fine, happy and pain free. They let me know that they were here. No words were spoken, only an instantaneous exchange of thoughts and feelings, like when speaking telepathically with animals. Each time, I recognized them in their formless, luminous bodies. The essence or energy signature of a person or animal does not change after life. It is the only thing that is permanent. We are eternal.

The all-encompassing warmth and love that my cats and my mother's presences radiated not only took my grief away but satiated all desire for physical contact. I felt filled with joy, and I woke up with a profound sense of peace and an expansive, deeply felt knowing that life does not die. We are all connected in this vast

---

[4]   Remote Viewing, widely used for espionage in the military, is a means that allows one to psychically access information and data from the target site. The viewers do not know what the target site is and are only given a set of numbers, or coordinates, that serve as a link connecting the subconscious mind to the target site—a remarkable demonstration of the illusion of space and time, and the communication and interconnectedness that is possible within the Unified Field.

cosmic web, a unified field, where our connections never cease. I stopped grieving, once I knew my mom and my cats were safe, happy and whole.

This deep-loving presence came again. Working as a volunteer counselor for the Pasadena Rape Hotline, I often found myself engulfed in the women's pain. Tossing with insomnia one evening, I curled in the fetal position bawling in the dark. Suddenly this gentle presence descended from my head downward into every cell of my body. Instantly, my mental anguish dissolved as this comforting flood of kindness and understanding washed through me. I wondered if it was my mom again, and where she found the fairy dust. I thanked whoever it was. I knew I was never alone. All of us have helpers.

As a child, I was afraid to fall asleep. Sometimes I'm still afraid to let go. My experiences of expanded awareness have depended entirely on my willingness to surrender and trust. One afternoon while I was taking a nap I heard faint, but annoying, sounds of metal clanking. As I placed my attention on the sound it became louder, and I realized this noise was coming from within. While the clanking reached a deafening crescendo, a progression of goosebumps mushroomed from my feet to my head and escalated into sweeping waves of bliss through my body. As I let go of my fear (of going crazy), I merged with the sound and lost body-consciousness. Boundaries between myself and my surroundings disappeared as I integrated with everything. I expanded into this fullness of love and wholeness, which was both ethereal and familiar, and that brought forth a downpour of tears. Thinking had stopped for those brief moments and, reflecting back, I realized how thought kept us bound to our bodies. Awareness was void of thought and had no boundaries. It seemed that if we could let go of ego-driven fear we might experience the higher frequencies of love.

One time this peaceful state remained for an entire day, and life felt like a wonderland. My surroundings appeared vibrant, luminous and magical. The trees and plants brimmed with life. I felt relaxed and weightless and bursting with aliveness and joy. Afterwards I would only experience this sporadically and for a short time, sometimes when I was meditating, practicing yoga or Kun Lun[5], or in the presence of awakened teachers and friends. I only wish I could feel its presence more often. Perhaps I simply need to ask and stay open to receive.

I know that we are more than our bodies, minds and thoughts. We are part of the unified field—a compassionate, all-seeing, omnipresent and benevolent presence. It is who we truly are. It speaks loudly when we need to hear it and grabs our attention in any way it can. So I knew my mom was saying hello when her favorite succulent, a Christmas cactus, which only blooms once a year, fully blossomed with radiant red flowers the day after she died. When we leave our bodies we drop our boundaries and merge with this presence. In a sense, we return to our roots—the unified field, or God.

I met Ernesto at the Self-Realization Fellowship as I was writing this book. We shared stories about our loved ones returning to us in dreams. Ernesto told me that he had found the remains of his beloved cat, who was eaten by a coyote. He and his wife planted a bright red poinsettia plant on the cat's grave. The next day, the plant had also fully blossomed and was glowing with spirit. Later, Ernesto dreamt of a big, toothy smile, and immediately recognized his cat's energy. "Can you imagine that?" Ernesto gleamed. "A smile from the other side!"

---

[5]   An ancient method of spiritual awakening

If we make soul contracts before we take birth, perhaps we choose the manner in which we die, including the circumstances and time. From what I have gathered from talking to animals who have passed on, it seems as though we continue on without our bodies.

Bailey, a handsome, large-built but delicate gray dog, told me he died at age fifteen shortly after his hips gave out. He said that he now was running by the ocean and visiting a blond-haired man who lived in an old, two-story, brown house. His person, Dana, said all of this was spot on, and that her uncle—a man who did not know Bailey— was dying. He had blond hair, before it turned gray, and lived in an old, two-story, brown house. Was Bailey preparing to meet Dana's dying uncle on the other side?

Our Purpose Continues

Maya was sorry that she hadn't been there for her dog, Flash, when he passed. She wanted to know if he had been ready to die, or if he had felt forced to leave his body. He was three years old. She also wanted to know what he was doing now on the other side. I asked Maya not to tell me how Flash died, because I preferred to hear it from her dog.

I asked Flash to show me which organs or body-parts were affected at the time of his death. Instantly I felt a full, swollen stomach and sensed bleeding from that area. At first I thought Flash may have had an aggressive, fast-growing tumor, but then I saw an image of people standing over him, and I wondered if he had been hit by a car. It seemed that Flash went quickly, and he didn't suffer.

Flash told me that he didn't die alone and showed me a blond, fair-skinned woman who helped him to cross over. He told me to tell Maya to not beat herself up, because there was nothing she could have done. I felt a huge flood of forgiveness from Flash and a willingness to let go. He had not felt forced to leave his body. He showed me an image of himself in the afterlife: patrolling, greeting or helping humans in some way on the other side. It seemed that Flash was a leader or of service in some way.

Maya confirmed that Flash had been hit by a car and had died ten minutes later. She had been there with him, and so was the man who hit him. When everyone had dispersed, Maya ran to tell people that Flash would be alright, but when she returned to Flash's side, Flash was dead.

Because Flash had been a skittish, nervous dog around humans, almost everyone had been afraid of him. Except Ms. Maggie, Flash's pet sitter, who had thought Flash was a wonderful dog. Maya wondered if Ms. Maggie was the one who helped Flash to cross over, since she was the only fair-skinned, blond haired woman that Maya knew of who had died.

What Maya and I found interesting was Flash's service work on the other side. Maya said that she had been planning to train Flash to be a service dog, so that he could go everywhere with her. I was certain that Flash was fulfilling his life's purpose.

The Caretaker

Lena, a German Shepherd, showed me an ocean and a beach where she played and ran. Then she showed me herself on a farm. Marta wanted to know if her dog, Lena, was with her other two dogs who passed before her. To my surprise, the answer was no! Lena said she had seen them, but that they were on different levels. Lena said she was busy care-taking.

I asked, "Taking care of what?"

Lena replied, "Herding sheep."

While this sounded ludicrous to me, I have learned to trust the information I receive and hold nothing back. Marta cried. She said Lena loved the ocean and that she and her husband often took Lena sheep herding! It was Lena's favorite thing to do.

Animals view death differently than we do. They don't have the attachments or regrets about not having done what they wanted to. When we resist what is, when we grieve and grasp at keeping our animals alive, we make passing much harder for them. While still in their physical bodies, our animals will hold on long as possible so that we do not have to bear life without them. Usually, when animals hear from their people that it is all right to leave their bodies, they will do so shortly after. When the time comes, give your animals permission to die.

Let Me Go, I'm Ready

Marge had a hard time letting go of her German Shepherd, Hogan. Hogan could no longer walk, and Marge knew she would probably have to euthanize him soon, but she wasn't certain that Hogan was ready to leave his body. She didn't want to end his life if he was not in pain.

When I arrived Hogan was strapped in diapers, and his massive body occupied half the bed. Hogan said he could no longer protect Marge in his present condition. He wanted to run in the back yard, but could not. He felt he was a burden. Although Hogan did not appear to be in pain, I did an energetic scan and was surprised to find his body heaving in severe discomfort, razor sharp in the hips. Although Hogan was ready to go, he had been hiding his agony for Marge's peace of mind. He welcomed assistance.

I am not certain if animals want assistance or whether they pick up the thought from us. I knew Marge was not going to let her dog lie there suffering, and yet the decision to terminate the dog's life had been a difficult one. I asked Marge if she was willing to give Hogan permission to go. It is important to let our animals know they can leave, and that we will be all right without them. Marge didn't want Hogan to hang on any longer than he needed to. She told Hogan to leave when he was ready, and that she would be fine.

Now that Hogan's feelings had been expressed and he knew that Marge would be all right, he finally let go. That evening, Hogan tossed, turned, moaned, and whimpered, displaying his discomfort and misery for the first time. Marge no longer had any doubt and knew what she had to do.

For all the joy they bring us, we owe it to our companions to make their passing as easy and worry-free as possible. My semi-feral cat Bootsie had gagged and drooled for one year while two vets convinced me the cause was either inflammation or a harmless polyp in the back of his throat. My own throat had burned while I mentally scanned Bootsie's body. I could not stop coughing and choking. Despite my concerns that something was seriously wrong with Bootsie, both vets ignored my unconventional findings. I finally sat in silence with Boots and, with sincere, determined intention, I said out loud to my guides, "Show me now what is wrong with my cat." In the next moment it seemed as if invisible hands were guiding my own hands—right where they needed to be. I found the cancer too late. The right side of his throat was as hard as a rock, and the vets later confirmed that the "harmless polyp" inside his throat was squamous cell carcinoma, which now had grown to one inch in diameter. No wonder he was gagging.

Even though Bootsie was dying, he was still hungry and incredibly thirsty, but he couldn't swallow, and now he was drooling blood. Even though I had given him pain killers, he was miserable.

While waiting for the vet to arrive to help Bootsie pass painlessly, I consulted another animal communicator. She knew nothing about me. She told me Bootsie wanted to reminisce about the good times we had shared. Bootsie told her that he loved to feel his head cupped in my hands, and that he wanted me to do that for him now. Being semi-feral, Mr. Boots, as I sometimes called him, never allowed me to hold him. Cupping his head in my hands is something he always allowed me to do. He then added, "Tell Diana to take her healing hands out into the world."

After we hung up I sang to Mr. Boots, and we reminisced. Bootsie began to purr. He enjoyed the review of his past and being told how special he was to me. He felt reassured that we would always be together. In the end animals want us to celebrate their lives.

After Bootsie died I took my healing practice public.

Say It Like You Mean It

The most painful part of losing our animals (and human companions) is watching them lose the "quality of their life." We wonder if it is time to put our animals down, or if we even should put them down. We are afraid to end their lives too soon, and we are afraid not to end their lives soon enough. When is the right time? We would prefer to see them go naturally, but we do not want to see them suffer. We are often too distraught to know which decision is best, and sometimes we are too emotional to hear what our animals want. Every road presents a difficult journey.

Rose's voice sounded too calm when she called to tell me that her twenty-three year old Apple Head Chihuahua, Taco, was dying. She told me she planned to euthanize her dog that afternoon.

Taco was still accepting food from a syringe, but she could barely stand up. Her breathing was labored, and Rose was certain that her dog was suffering. I asked Rose if she was ready to let Taco go. They had been inseparable since the day Rose rescued Taco from a freeway in Texas, when the dog was thirteen years old. She was quick to respond to my question with a "Yes, yes. I am ready to let Taco go."

When I tuned into Taco, I didn't feel that she was quite ready to go. There was something she was waiting for, but I was not exactly sure what this was. Her body felt achy and uncomfortably stiff like cardboard, but I did not pick up severe pain. Taco was not suffering, and I suggested that Rose wait before euthanizing her.

I asked Rose if she had given Taco permission to die, and if she had reminisced about the good times she had with her dog. Rose said yes, that she had told Taco to leave when she was ready, but that they had not yet celebrated their lives together.

I did a healing for both of them over the phone, taking Rose into a deep, restful space—a space that allows our animals to also be at peace, and a space allowing both human and animal to completely surrender. Later that evening Rose told Taco how much she meant to her, and she recalled the good times that they had shared together. I knew that Taco would pass soon, yet there was a missing link. Something else needed to come forth.

The very next morning Rose felt a huge shift inside, as if the small self had stepped aside and allowed a greater strength to step forth. A compassionate self that wanted what was best for her companion. Now she truly was ready to let go of her dog and was determined to stop her dog's suffering. She looked at Taco and meant what she said. "I don't want to see you like this. I am calling the vet right now to help you pass."

She texted her sister to tell her what she was doing. Her sister texted back, "where are you taking her?" And then in that instant, with the phone still in her hands and her dog still under her shirt and snuggled against her chest, Rose felt Taco take one deep breath, exhale and leave her body. Our animals try to hang on until we are ready to let go. Telling them that it's all right to leave their bodies is not always enough. We have to mean it.

Rose later shared something special. She told me that when I described what I had felt during my body scan for Taco, that I had described exactly how she, Rose, had been feeling for the past three weeks. Rose said her joints ached every day, and her body felt stiff just like cardboard. She didn't think much of it until Taco died. Rose said she woke up the following morning, after her dog had passed, expecting to feel the same aches and stiffness she had felt for the last three weeks, but to her surprise all the aches were gone.

Before working with Rose and Taco, I had not realized that we humans can feel our animal's physical ailments in our own bodies, just as our animals can mirror our ailments in their bodies. I suppose anything is possible when we love each other, and our bonds are deep.

Tomasita's Last Night

Three months to live. Eight months maximum. Leda would not accept the death sentence that the vet gave her dog. Tomasita was only six years old, and this little Chihuahua had a promising career ahead of her. She was a therapy dog, and her heartfelt, humorous character changed peoples' lives. Tomasita visited children's hospitals, homes for the elderly and comforted the terminally ill. Tomasita was helping humanity. People counted on her to brighten their day.

When Tomasita suddenly stopped eating, Leda took her in for tests. This is when Leda found out that Tomasita's lymph nodes were flooded with cancer. Leda couldn't bear the thought of losing her girl, her favorite, loving companion. Tomasita was the only one who she could cradle in her arms like a baby, and she was the gentlest and smartest of Leda's animal family.

Leda was devastated. This was her first animal to be terminally diagnosed. She could not imagine life without Tomasita, and she cried day and night. She researched both conventional and alternative treatments and started a medicinal protocol for her dog immediately.

Healings seemed to help both Leda and her dog, and by the end of five days Tomasita was eating again. The vet found Leda's dog to be more present, energetic and responsive. Leda shifted into a positive mind state and was convinced that Tomasita would get through this.

When things like this crash our world, we place our priorities in order. Leda did some soul searching. She told me she had spent hours, possibly ten to twelve hours every day, on the computer answering emails from the children. She wrote letters to directors of facilities so Tomasita could continue to help others. All of this continuous correspondence required Leda's constant attention. Leda's life, her entire days and nights, were consumed with work and, she confided, "It is making me sick."

Although Leda was not physically sick, her Tomasita was gravely ill. In one short day Leda realized that none of what she had been doing was important anymore. What was important was her life with her family and the time she shared with her animal companions, especially with Tomasita. Leda announced that she was through with all the superficial distractions that she had created around her life.

She decided to spend quality time with those nearest to her. Those who truly cared and loved her. She realized how fragile life was, how one's health can crumble in a snap, and how important it was to be here. Now. Being with her dog and her cats, watching them play and sitting in her beautiful Mexican garden with the birds and squirrels had always given Leda the most peace and inspiration. She knew now what she had to do. Return to joy.

I took a peek at the emotional causes of lymph node issues. I already knew that holding on to resentment and grief can "eat away" at the self, and cancer can manifest in the body. What I read about the emotional causes behind lymph node issues did not surprise me: *A warning that the mind needs to be re-centered on the essentials of life. Love and joy.*

Leda viewed Tomasita's cancer as a wake-up call—the slap that she needed to direct herself back to the essentials in life. Tomasita's love alone had filled Leda's soul to the brim. Tomasita had much to share and much to teach Leda, and this special dog was too young to die. Leda had a mission to fulfill. She made up her mind to return to the simple life that made her truly happy. She would heal her dog, and she would change her life forever.

As time progressed, Tomasita's condition did not improve, but it did not get worse. Leda continued to shower her dog with love and positive thoughts while holding an enthusiastic intention for Tomasita to heal. Although death was a possibility, Leda refused to allow this possibility into her conscious mind. "Tomasita will be healed." Leda repeated these words to herself and anticipated a cancer-free body. I continued to send healing energy to Tomasita every day and to visualize her already healed. The healings relaxed Tomasita, and her breathing became less labored.

Three weeks passed. One early morning Tomasita slammed her body up against Leda while she was sleeping and woke her up. Leda heard roosters crowing over the blanket of dawn while she pet her dog in the wee hours. Those magical hours when our minds are undisturbed by thought and seem to hover gently in the darkness that surrounds us. Perhaps it was because Leda was half asleep that she became receptive to spontaneous Divine guidance and found herself speaking from the heart. She heard herself saying words to her dog that had never entered her mind before. And in that moment she meant them. "Mi Tomasita, I love you so much. If you need to go, then go. Mamasita will survive." At that moment Tomasita's breathing became smooth and easy.

Tomasita then rested her head on Leda's chest and placed her paw on Leda's cheek. Then Tomasita took one deep breath, as though savoring her last bite of life, and released a long, relaxed exhale and passed away.

During Tomasita's last week of life, I was distracted and felt resistance when I tried to send healing to her, and I didn't know why. Tomasita knew that she was losing her life force and was no longer accepting the healing. She was preparing to leave and had waited for the right moment, a harmonious alignment—when Leda was perfectly receptive and willing to let go. Yet only for that brief moment, when Leda, quite unwittingly, stepped aside, was Leda willing to let go.

Now, her unconscious surrender seemed like a cruel joke. She felt deeply betrayed by God. She had never asked for a miracle before. Just this one time. She asked that Tomasita be healed. Death appeared from nowhere, trampling over her prayers and ripping a huge hole in Leda's heart.

When it is our time to die, no healing or remedy will work. It seems that when the soul's work is finished, it will leave the body. What appears to us as untimely death could be the beginning of a deeper journey for that soul. We may feel that an animal or person is "too young" to die, but what seems to us to be a short life span may be all the time that was needed for a particular soul to experience what it came here to experience in a physical body.

Everything in life, including our death, may be perfectly timed, and embedded in our contract. Although these thoughts are never intended to comfort anyone who is devastated by the death of a loved one. The pain is always unbearable. Only our sleep swallows our loss—for a while—until grief and despair greet us again in the morning, taking us on their own journey into a deeper, uncharted part of ourselves.

Gone Like A Rocket

I was stunned when the vet told me Baba Looie was dying. He was my first animal to go, and I was not ready to release him. Grief struck, and I forgot to talk about the good times we had together. He had tremendous anxiety about leaving. Most likely, he internalized my sadness and resistance and held on until the last possible moment.

Baba Looie delivered the death wail at dawn. He found strength to stumble across the room to my bedside and not die alone. After about twenty minutes of heavy breathing, Baba's spirit left his body with such force that it slammed him a few inches back against the wall. Shocked, I dropped his paw and fell back in the opposite direction. Baba looked electrified by the jolt and left with his eyes wide open, his body stiffed in a straight line and his arms flung overhead. Perhaps death comes more easily when we do not resist.

Lighten Up! I'm Only Dying

Amanda, a thirteen-year-old Rottweiler, wanted to reminisce on her final day. Amanda told me her person, Kelly, rode horses and had recently changed jobs. She also confided other secrets that only she and Kelly shared. Amanda felt her heart and mind were still young and vibrant, although she knew her body was ready to go. Cancer-ridden, she could no longer walk and did not want to be carried downstairs to pee outside. Nor did she want to lie there all day. She wanted to run and dance. It was time to go. "The right thing to do."

Amanda continued to tell me about her favorite times with Kelly—swimming, going to the ocean, and to the ranch. She went on and on, giving Kelly closure and reassuring her person that euthanasia was all right with her. Kelly could do this now, knowing Amanda was happy, in full acceptance and not afraid.

Hey! Where's My Green Ball?

Siri, a Russian Wolfhound, was dying of cancer. One leg had already been amputated in an attempt to save his life, but the cancer had returned and spread to his lungs and other organs.

Now he had not eaten or walked in four days. His people, Jenny and Martin, finally decided to put him down over the weekend and hired me to ask Siri if this was what he wanted.

When I walked into Jenny's rustic, country home, I met a skinny, listless dog stretched across his doggie bed on the floor by the window. I didn't expect the entire family to hover over me, weeping, during the consultation. Martin, Jenny, her mother and father, their twelve-year-old son, and their back-house tenant filled the sofa and chairs, wiping tears away as they surrounded Siri and me on the floor.

Soon, I joined in—until I dried my eyes and blew my nose and finally got hold of myself.

Kneeling by Siri's side, I sent healing energy to him for about forty minutes. Even though an animal is dying, healing can still be beneficial, relaxing them, alleviating pain and allowing them to let go and surrender. Sometimes, healing will speed up the dying process. In other cases, it can improve their condition. I had nothing to lose.

After the healing, Siri had tons to say. He told me intimate details about the family, hilarious moments he remembered and things he loved doing. He addressed everyone in the room. As I recounted his stories to his extended family, everyone laughed hard and the atmosphere lightened. Siri wagged his tail! Siri then asked, "Where is my green ball?"

Jenny and Martin gasped as though they hit the jackpot twice. The green ball was Siri's all-time favorite toy, and it sat in the bed of Martin's truck. They had taken it away, thinking their dog was too weak to play.

When my session was over, Siri's entourage left the room grinning. About a half hour later, as I communicated to Jenny's other dog, Siri tried to stand on his skinny three legs. Martin flew in and almost tripped over Siri as he helped the dog get outdoors to pee. Yet Siri did not want to come back into the house. Martin fetched the green ball from the back of his pickup truck and threw it across the lawn. Everyone watched Siri romp like a puppy, chasing the ball around the front yard. I continued the healing and communications with him for three weeks as he regained his appetite and a zest for living. His family said he still played, pursuing his green ball across the lawn.

The cancer progressed, despite the supplements, love, and healing given. Yet Jenny and Martin had found closure in those extra special weeks, and Siri chose to pass on his own, without any fuss or muss and without assistance. At three o'clock in the morning, Martin heard Siri scrambling to climb onto the couch. As Martin went to assist his dog, Siri stood up on his own. He pointed his long nose toward the ceiling. He yelped one, howling death call. Siri's body collapsed onto the floor, and his spirit left his body.

Accidental Death?

Bella was killed instantly when a car slammed into her body on a rainy, black New Year's Eve. Driving home from a twenty-four hour Tara chant at the Tibetan Buddhist Temple, I spotted only the tail end of the sailing car that left Bella flapping in the middle of the road. I understand animals, but I don't understand humans. She was a large boned, long legged animal, who would have had to have made a loud thump. I blocked traffic by parking my car in front of her.

Our eyes met for a quick moment before she died in my arms. So many feelings are spoken in one quick glance. Bella looked stunned and scared, and did not know what had hit her. Another practitioner driving home from the Temple stopped his car to help me drag Bella off the four-lane road in the downpour.

In Los Angeles, the sanitation department picks up dead animals, and the bodies are brought to the rendering plant. At the time, I was informed that neither department had the time to call the phone numbers on the tags or to even remove the collars. The animals were minced into meat with their collars intact. I had a hunch that Bella had loving humans. I wanted them to be notified, and I did not want Bella rendered into pet food. I removed her collar, and on New Years Day I called her people.

Diana DelMonte

That evening, Bella's people did find her body where I had left it. It turned out the mother and two children were from out of state, visiting their in-laws. A relative had left the gate open, and Bella had trotted down the street to the main road, stepping right out in front of a passing car.

Bella's family was heartbroken, yet the woman saw a blessing behind the tragedy. Bella was an old gal who had recently been diagnosed with carcinoma in her organs. Perhaps a quick death was better than a prolonged, painful one with difficult decisions to face. I wondered if Bella might have known exactly what she was doing.

Maharji says, "No one dies before their time or stays one moment after." When the spirit is ready to leave the body, there will be a cause to make it happen. There are no accidents, and no one is to blame. Divine order governs the stars, the planets, our bodies, our lives, our journey here, and our death. If we hold on to guilt, blame, and the what-ifs, then we do not allow and accept the what-is.

Our thoughts affect our animals, both the living and those who have made their transitions. If our animals want us to be happy, they certainly do not want their deaths to destroy our lives. They do not want us to live in sorrow and unforgivable regret. Our attachment creates suffering, in this life and the next.

Death jolts all of us into remembering, even for a moment, the impermanence of our lives. We are taken into the present moment, into the here-and-now of ourselves. Our animals live here—in the center of their hearts, and they keep them open for us. Their death brings humility and graciousness into our lives. We experience the bittersweet vibrancy of life as we connect to our inwardness and our aliveness, which is so necessary for spiritual growth.

Brownie

Brita contacted me again from Sweden to ask why her cat Brownie had to die so young. Brownie was only two years old when he was killed by a car. I had no answers for Brita. I tuned into Brownie. He told me he was caught off guard and did not expect to die at that moment, but once he "floated away," he knew he was perfectly fine. He said that he didn't need to experience illness or old age, and that he had important things to do now. Brownie said that he had come into Brita's life to show her something.

Then I received an image of Brownie as a happy, human child, running and laughing. I had a clear feeling that he had been a child in other lifetimes, and that he may have died young in those lifetimes as well. I felt as if Brownie might continue to be born and continue to die at a young age, until he felt ready to live out his life to maturity. I wondered if we really did make these choices before birth.

While I had absolutely no way of knowing if any of this was true, my words did resonate with Brita. She said Brownie was always child-like and never grew up. She said Brownie's voice, his small, rounded face and his personality had not changed since he was six months old. She said she had always thought that, "time had stopped for Brownie and that he stopped growing, as he continued to meow and play like a kitten."

Brita did not believe in accidents and felt that all of us are here to do something important in our lives. She believed that we are here to help others and our planet. Brita thought about Brownie's child-like essence and wondered if kindred spirits might be waiting for us to have children, so they could be born. She had chosen not to be a mother. She wondered what Brownie's message to her could have been.

Brita said she had rescued a pregnant mom two years ago, who she named Lida. Lida had one kitten, Brownie. Since kitten-hood, he had showered Brita with gentleness and love. She recalled all the years, before Brownie, that she spent in sadness and depression. Now Brita was determined to not waste a single moment. She decided to finish the children's book that she had started writing years ago. Our animals always seem to spur us into action.

My Message To You

Death is certain. When death will come, is not.

Six years had passed since I worked with Dali's separation anxiety issues. During this time, he had brought his person, Carol, through a deep, inner-healing journey. Dali had later become a well-behaved and emotionally balanced show dog.

Now Dali had recently been diagnosed with an inoperable cancer on his spleen. It was pushing against his kidneys, which were operating at forty percent capacity. Dali was weak and exhausted some days, and other days he was vigorous and enthusiastic. Carol didn't know whether Dali was healing, or hanging on for some specific purpose. She asked me to tune in and find out.

Dali had an enormous glow of light around him, but I didn't know if this light was his physical life-force, or his vibrant spirit. He felt fragile as a water bubble, ready to slip away at any moment. And yet, although I felt burning in his stomach, this area felt solid and compact, as though this growth inside of him was getting smaller. I asked Dali if he was healing. Or was he hanging on to finish his work?

This is what I heard; "I have done what I came here to do. If I stay on, it is to have fun and enjoy life with Carol. What else is there to do?"

"What was your purpose in Carol's life?"

"I think Carol knows that answer. She has fulfilled her creative side. My showmanship is hers, too. We are partners here. I have made her so proud of me, given her a sense of well-being, and this has given purpose to her life. She is proud now too and holds her head high. She has entered a new phase in her life. My agility and performance requires presence. This is what it's all about; being present with who you are. Just being yourself. Carol is more herself now. Tell Carol not to fall if I leave. She must continue to hold her head high. This is what it's about. This is my message. This is my purpose in her life. Tell her not to cry. Move out from the center. This is what my performance is about. This is how I am able to do what I have done. I am happy to be alive. Let's just take things from here. We will always walk together. Lets's take it from there."

This sounded like a farewell message, but I felt that Dali still had some time. I sent Dali's message to Carol in an Mp3 format, since I had no time to call her. She listened to the recording with Dali that morning. He died shortly afterwards. Perhaps Dali joined his father, who had passed just two days before. Life seems to fall in step at the right time.

An Angel Brings Death

Watching my animals die did not make the process any easier. I was always frantic when my animals were dying—until an angel crossed my path. I had never seen this small, gray, feral cat in my yard before, until she walked right out in front of me one day in the pouring rain. I was darting to my friend's truck in the driveway to work with her elderly dog, who was too weak to get out of the vehicle. The phantom feline appeared out of nowhere, mewing. She was drenched. I put her in my bathroom and went to work with the dog.

An hour later, I returned to Angel and patted her dry. I took her to the vet, who suggested euthanasia. But I refused, thinking I could

95

bring her around. Back home, I trimmed her long claws, which had curled in ghastly long spirals. Her breath smelled like rancid meat. I knew feral cats approached humans when they were sick. But if she wasn't feral, why was she dying alone outdoors? And why had she come to me?

I made a bed for Angel. She immediately climbed onto the soft, warm pillows and let out a long sigh, as though she was home. She never moved again. Her body grew cool as her life force dwindled. Within a few short hours, her breathing labored. I sat with Angel for most of the night, held her paw, and sang to her. I told her how beautiful she was. She was dead by morning.

Angel presented dying to me in a new way—with presence and acceptance. No blame, no guilt. She taught me how to sit with death without attachment and in true compassion. I learned from her to be here with each moment, to feel the subtle intertwine of life and death, their sadness and joy. The door is thin. As Lisa Mora says, it's as fragile as life itself. Angel enabled me to be present for Bootsie's passing and for my Dad when he took his last breath.

The Last Wink

My mom squeezed my hand and never opened her eyes the entire time. When she loosened her grip, I said good-bye. It was time to go home. I don't know why I left my mom in that hospital bed to die alone, but thirty-one years later I had one request; that I be present when my Dad took his last breath.

He had been gasping for air before Hospice gave him a morphine drip. Now his breath rate was down to twelve breaths a minute. Twenty-six breaths a minute were normal. Thanks to my yoga practice, I slowed my breathing to match my father's. I sat at the edge of his bed breathing with him, inhaling and exhaling in this slow, rhythmic cycle. His eyes were closed shut. I wondered if he was aware that I was there. I put on the music that I had always played for him when I did energy-work. Now he knew for certain that I was with him in the room. Not even five minutes passed when I heard the death rattle. I leaned over him and touched his arm. Ready to leave his body, my dad took two, long, deep breaths and as he inhaled his third and final breath, and while under the strong sedation of morphine, he managed to open his left eye for a quick second and look straight at me. Taken aback, I said, "Bye dad." He shut his eye, exhaled and left his body. Perhaps my dad was saying, "Everything is all right honey. I'm going now. Not a big deal." Death was the ultimate surrender and, as some spiritual teachers have said, it was like taking off a tight shoe.

Until We Meet Again, Enjoy the Ride!

You will know when it's time for your animal to leave. Unless it's a sudden death, your animals will let you know when it's time, whether they want help or want to pass on their own. Listen to your hunches.

Friends thought I was selfish for not euthanizing Yudi, my fifteen-year-old cat. Yudi had either a brain tumor or a neurological disorder, quite possibly FIP, the dry form of the virus which attacks the nerves. One year earlier, shortly after Baba's death, I had noticed Yudi had a slight facial twitch. I knew then that I was going to lose him. Slowly, his disorder progressed until he was disoriented and paced the perimeter of the rooms. He had told me he could no longer see well. Perhaps now he was totally blind.

One day, I returned home and couldn't find him. I lived in one room. Finally, I spotted him pinned between the bed and the wall. Apparently, Yudi could not back up or continue forward. The space was narrow, and he had met an obstacle—a pillow on the floor in his pathway. I found my poor fellow with his jaw locked around a chunk of the pillow. His heart pounded like a steel drum as I pried his mouth open to release the pillow. He drank bowls of water afterwards. I had no idea how long he had been stuck. I'd been gone for hours.

Yudi never stopped pacing. His eyes no longer shut but remained glazed open. Every time I asked him if he wanted help to leave his body, I heard "No, my job is not done yet." Confused, I consulted a colleague and psychic, Marina.

"Yudi is not ready to leave," she confirmed. "His work isn't finished."

One afternoon, Yudi and I sat in each other's arms rocking in the breeze under the Meyer lemon tree in my ivy-covered backyard in Los Feliz, on the east side of Los Angeles. Perhaps it was Yudi who prompted me to ask. "Who were you in my past lifetime?" Never before had I asked anyone this question. Although I believed in reincarnation, I had never been interested enough to delve further. I was more interested in the present.

Yudi's unexpected answer gave me the closure I needed to let go. He flashed me a clear, vivid picture of himself as an Eastern Indian man dressed in white. He had his arm around me. I was also dressed in white. Since an image is delivered with emotions, thoughts and feelings, a deeper meaning surfaced. Yudi had been my spiritual teacher, and I was his student. Our work had not been completed, and we continued together on our spiritual paths in this lifetime. I felt the jump of unspoken truth settle in my gut.

I asked Yudi why he came back as a cat.

"To open your heart," he replied.

What better way to open a human heart than to take rebirth as an animal. Animals have no ego, no agenda, nothing to achieve, and no reason to excel, argue, or compete. They can simply be and demonstrate unconditional love, forgiveness, and deep joy.

I still could not end my little Guru's life, so I went back to my colleague, Marina. I told her nothing. I simply asked, "Is it time now?" Marina held him like a baby for quite a long time, feeling his energy and receiving his thoughts. He sunk into her arms. I sunk into the comforting silence. Then Marina shocked me.

"He was a man..." she said. "An Indian man." I nearly fell off her couch. "Yes," she continued, "he is ready now." A few days later, Yudi went into death seizures. When he whimpered and violently shook, I asked the vet to help him pass.

We have our soul contracts and are here helping each other to evolve. Our lives do not begin at birth and end at death. Our experiences and relationships with one another, human and animal, far surpass this lifetime. Animals who choose to live with us—those that show up at our doorstep, those we take in or adopt, those we stop to rescue off the street or save from death at the pound—are kindred souls.

I found my cat Ertha when she was two-months-old. Despite the deep bond that instantly blossomed between us, I advertised to find a home for her. I simply had too many cats. But I never had a female. And I had never known a cat to perch on my shoulder like a bird or one who loved to be photographed. Besides this, I had already named her. I suppose any reason becomes a good reason to bring another homeless animal into your life. I ended up keeping her.

One evening, years later, I dreamt that I was married to a wonderful, kind man. The dream was so vivid that I could still recall his face in my mind. He had fine features, a slender build and was of average height. His hair was light brown, his demeanor was gentle, and he loved me so much. We were laughing as we walked arm in arm through a town or village. Waking up for quick moments throughout the night, I felt this man's presence next to me in bed. Then I would slip back into the dream, back to my husband. In the morning, still in the twilight of sleep and still feeling his strong presence next to me, I turned to embrace him. I was stunned to find Ertha laying next to me. Yes, perhaps this sound nuts, and yes, you probably already know what I'm about to say. I can't help but wonder if Ertha might have been my husband in a past life. After all, one can only know such things through one's heart.

Know that you will meet your companions again, if not in this lifetime, then in the next. Pay attention to your dreams. Pay attention to who you're drawn to. Pay attention to who crosses your path. Your animals may or may not return in the form that you expect. But you will always recognize them, no matter what form they take.

CHAPTER 8

WHY ANIMALS LEAVE HOME— MISSING ANIMALS

There are no accidents.
Anything you perceive to be a challenge,
problem or crisis is a blessing in disguise.
You need to look at it in a different way.

J.D. Messinger,
11 Days in May: The Conversation
That Will Change Your Life

T he bulk of my calls are for lost animals. It is heartbreaking when animals never return home. Some are killed by cars, coyotes or cruel people. Some are stolen or find new homes. Others seem to vanish in thin air. People pick up dogs and refuse to give them back, or they find cats in their yard and relocate them. Yet those that do return make my services the most rewarding.

Our companions leave home for many reasons. Some are bored, especially indoor cats or dogs who never leave the yard. Animals have an intelligent curiosity and want to explore the world, just as we do. Yet outdoor cats are sometimes bullied off their turf and become afraid to return. Sometimes they have run so far that they become disoriented and cannot find their way back, or they have found a safe place and do not wish to venture home. People leave on vacation, and their animal slips past the pet sitter and out the door. Some get trapped in sheds and garages. Cats who run off are often close by, but they're too afraid to answer your calls or have jumped a fence and cannot jump back.

Dogs leave for similar reasons. They want to explore the neighborhood, or they want exercise or do not like being left home alone. Gardeners leave the gate open. One dog walked out of her gated property down the steep hill. Because she had hip dysplasia, she could not walk back up the incline. If an animal-loving person had not spent twenty minutes coaxing this dog into her car, the dog would have remained lost on the streets.

Some animals go off to die. But in more cases, our companions leave because of chaos or abuse in their home. It takes their absence for us to turn our lives around.

I'll Be Home In One Week

Buster was in indoor cat who bolted the first chance he got. He did not intend to stay away forever—he just needed some time to himself. His person, Cindy, and her partner argued all the time. Buster told me he needed to regain his equilibrium.

"Things are topsy turvy in the house," he said. "I'll be home in a week."

Unfortunately, Buster never made it back home and was never seen again. Buster's disappearance led Cindy to the local shelter. She now volunteers there once a week, working with the dogs and bottle-feeding orphaned kittens. Currently, she has five little ones at her home.

"Because of you," Cindy said, "I became interested in animal communication. And while I can't do what you do, just knowing that it is possible has made it so much easier to listen to the animals. It makes my work at the shelter so fulfilling. I definitely pick up on each animal's energy, and that allows me to understand more of what they need at the moment. It has also made me more aware of my own energy and how it affects those around me. I am okay with everything. Buster is somewhere, either in his earthly body or as pure energy, and I am happy knowing that. So thank you. This entire experience really has been life-changing."

Life can be cruel and unfair, but if we can find the strength to roll with our circumstances, we may find our lives redirected, and ourselves growing in a completely different way and living for a completely different purpose. One thing is certain; we'll create less suffering for ourselves.

I Can't Stand It Anymore

Brenda was stuck. We've all been there—working a job or staying in a relationship that no longer serves us. Making excuses, ignoring our hunches, and not looking fear in the face. It takes a sweet, loving animal to get us to do what is right for ourselves. This is why Pedro left.

While I was focused primarily on locating Brenda's cat, Pedro, I forgot to ask him why he left and if he even wanted to be found! If an animal does not wish to return, I cannot make them appear with my magic wand. I gave Brenda a description of Pedro's surroundings and did my best to determine if he was injured or even still alive.

Then I dowsed[6] for a direction and distance away from Brenda's home. I continued to track Pedro. Since he was not showing up and there were no sightings, I asked a colleague to double-check to see if Pedro was truly alive. The door is thin, the transition subtle, and life force is sometimes difficult to determine. Sometimes, animals do not realize they are dead.

My colleague immediately heard one sentence loud and clear: "I can't stand it anymore!" This slipped my mind and I did not mention it to Brenda. Meanwhile, I found Pedro's heart center was closed. I sensed turmoil back at the home and asked Brenda to tell me what was going on. Brenda said she supported her father-in-law and worked long restaurant hours that required a four-hour train commute into Boston. Unhappy, Pedro peed in the house. The father-in-law isolated him to one room, which made Pedro more upset. Yet this was the past. Pedro no longer was confined, and Brenda was home more now. She was devastated that Pedro was not returning.

During one phone session, Brenda told me the truth. In tears, she told me she had an opportunity to move to a farm to care-take the grounds and the cats on the property. She could finally quit her job and have a peaceful environment. Yet she remained trapped in what she viewed to be a hopeless, stagnant situation. Her husband was in the military, and Brenda felt obligated to care for his father, an

---

[6] Dowsing is an ancient art where dowsing rods or pendulums are used to locate underground water, oil, minerals, archaeological artifacts and missing people. No one knows how it works but, since everything has an energy field, I believe the dowser establishes an energetic or vibratory connection with the sought item or missing animal. The rods or pendulum, held by the dowser, serve as an amplifier or antennae. Einstein's thoughts on this: "The dowsing rod is a simple instrument which shows the reaction of the human nervous system to certain factors which are unknown to us at this time."

abusive man with onset alzheizmer's, who was not fond of Brenda's cats. Brenda imagined herself free from all this and living alone with her felines on the farm, but could not step forward. She blurted, "I can't stand it anymore!"—Pedro's own thoughts!

Since Brenda could not take the step to leave, choosing instead to sacrifice her peace of mind, Pedro left.

Pedro's disappearance was a lightning bolt, the shock Brenda needed to get the ball rolling and leave a co-dependent, destructive relationship and to do what her soul and heart longed and needed to do. It was time to do the right thing for the highest good of everyone involved. She found someone who did cranio-sacral healing to release energetic blockages, and someone to care for her father-in-law. Then she moved, with all her cats, to a guesthouse on the farm. A few weeks after she was settled into a peaceful mind on the quiet farm, Pedro was found. Brenda believed that the healings "opened a space creating a path for Pedro to return."

One year later, her indoor/outdoor cat, Elliot, left. Although he came around every day to eat, he kept his distance and refused to come in. He would no longer even allow Brenda to touch him. This was a doting cat who had never left Brenda's side and sat on her lap every chance he got. Elliot had a sense of humor and made her laugh. Now he wanted nothing to do with Brenda, and for the past two weeks he no longer stopped by to eat.

Brenda was planning to buy a house and move to Vermont, since she had found the job of her dreams. These were not easy commitments. Her husband had three more years in Iraq. Brenda was overwhelmed and distraught with so many open ends in her life. Now she faced leaving the farm and leaving twenty outdoor cats that she had neutered and now fed—strays that the property owner acquired but neglected.

Brenda realized that the more she continued to clear her inner space and rid herself of fear, the more she was "clearing a path" for Elliot to come home. After we did some healing work over the phone, the cat was on her back porch the next day. "Elliot now sits on the window sill inside the house and lets me have his belly every morning. He lets me kiss him on the sill."

Shortly after Elliot returned, Marvin, an outdoor stray, left. He had been gone a few days, which was not unusual for him. The problem was that Brenda was leaving the farm in five days and did not want to leave Marvin behind. I told Brenda to send Marvin a mental picture of her leaving and an image of an empty house, and then to send Marvin a contrasting image of him going with her. I suggested she top it by telling him that, if this is what he wanted, he needed to show up now. Marvin returned the next morning.

Animals will make their own decisions. It helps to show them their options. They do understand. Felini certainly did. Having distemper as a kitten, Felini walked with a wobbly, crippled gate. Brenda did not want to leave him behind. She would have taken all twenty cats from the property if she could have. However, the property owner insisted that Felini stay on the farm, and the owner had the last word. But Felini had already stolen Brenda's heart, and as some of you may already know, when one has been struck delirious with kitty fever there is only one thing to do. Brenda told Felini that if he wanted to come with her, he needed to urinate in the woman's home. Two days went by when the woman of the property approached Brenda. "This damn cat! He's been spraying and urinating all over my house. You can have him!"

Brenda moved with Felini, Pedro, Marvin, Elliot and her other five cats to the newly purchased home in Vermont. She had only been there a month when Elliot dropped weight and lost his appetite and muscle control in his back legs. To Brenda's dismay, Elliot was diagnosed with the FIP virus. He must have known he was sick, and perhaps part of the reason he had left was to alert Brenda and prepare her for his final departure.

Let Me Go

William had only turned his head for a few moments when Molly vanished in the snow. His fifteen-year-old Australian Shepherd had dementia and her arthritis was worsening. William could not accept Molly's decline or the idea that she might be leaving her body soon.

I tracked Molly to a particular house on a hill nearby, where I learned she had also been sighted. However, Molly did not turn up, despite William's thorough search attempts. Thinking Molly was disoriented and could not find her way home, I asked her if she were lost and if I could enter her energy field to scan for injuries. She said, "Yes! I will do anything to make William realize that I am not coming back." Molly must have known how hard it was for her person to accept her physical deterioration. William never found Molly's body.

Animals know when it's time for their death, and sometimes they want to spare us the pain. Even though we would rather be with our companions when they leave their bodies, they sometimes choose, as Molly did, to do it their own way. Perhaps Elliot had second thoughts and decided to return to Brenda after she became more centered and better able to handle losing him, although none of us are ever truly ready.

You Drive Me Nuts

Baba Looie lived a double life—and yes, he had nine lives. Every person and every animal has their own way of handling stress. As I told you, Bubby sprayed for ten years. His long-haired brother, Baba Looie, took off every day. Gone from nine to five. I thought he had a job. Not being the best mom in the world, I didn't always know where my children were. I had no idea that Baba Looie hung out on the porch of my neighbor Phil's vacant apartment units. I never paid attention to the two shabby buildings down the hill from his house. I did not know that Phil even owned them or that my cat ventured down so close to the busy boulevard to sit on the porch.

My other neighbors, directly next door to the units, thought Baba was a stray. Fortunately, they didn't find him a home! Instead, they put out an old rug for my collarless boy and fed him every day. Baba had his secret routine: go by the neighbor's picture window to visit their indoor cat through the glass, wait to be fed, and then head over to his rug on the porch, to snooze and watch the traffic passing on Silverlake Boulevard all day. There was a peace on the porch that he did not find at home.

One evening, Baba didn't show up for dinner. He was still missing the next morning and the next evening and the day after that. I contacted an animal communicator, since I was not doing this work at the time—and even if I had been, I was too emotionally attached to have gotten a true reading. Jane, the communicator, described my neighbor Phil's house and the cars in his car port, although Phil denied that my cat could possibly be anywhere on his property. Baba Looie told Jane that he was extremely stressed at home and that even now, away from me and my partner, he still cringed at the thought of doors slamming and us fighting. Baba said that he liked us both, but when we were together, we created tension. I wondered if Jane could see my red face through the phone.

Three weeks passed. No Baba. What Jane had not told me was that Baba was trapped. He had fallen through the floorboards of the porch into a narrow closet inside the apartment and could not jump back out. He was starving to death as I continued my search up in the hills, never thinking of looking down toward the Boulevard below, even though the description of Phil's house and cars matched what Jane had seen.

Life unfolds in mysterious ways. While I packed my days with prayer, Phil decided to do some plumbing in one of the units—the very unit where Baba was trapped. My kitty, by the grace of God, came hobbling home. He was weak, dehydrated and skinny as a rail.

My partner and I tried not to argue in front of the cats. Yet, although we held back our outbursts, we could not hide our feelings or the tense, angry energy. To our animals and children, this kind of energy is a bomb.

Let Go, Let God

It wasn't until Betty let go that Harley was found, although it was too late. Betty was determined to find her rescued Husky who had escaped from the neighbor's yard when she was at work. It was Harley's second attempt. Betty hired a few of us to locate Harley, and we tracked him for months. He would not stop running.

Betty spent several months pounding the streets, notifying the town, the mail carriers and the UPS man. She posted signs, ran ads, and contacted the local newspaper and television stations. Although she was devastated by his disappearance, Betty had to let it go and redirect her focus to her other dog, who's health was now in a steep decline. By letting go and dropping the force and fight, Betty "cleared a pathway" allowing events to unfold in Divine timing.

In less than a week, Betty received a call from a couple. It was the first night that this man and woman had decided to turn off their noisy air conditioner. In the quiet night, they heard Harley whimpering in their backyard bushes.

Harley's emaciated body was infested with mange, and maggots had buried themselves into his flesh. His organs were failing. Betty gave the Emergency Animal Clinic permission to euthanize her dog.

When I work with missing animals, I have found that most people, although heartbroken, are thankful for whatever closure they can get. The universe seems to spare those who cannot bear that sort of closure and the pain of knowing. Their animals are never found. Although death may cross these persons' minds, they never drop their glimmer of hope.

Free Spirit

Two weeks after Georgiane moved into a new condo, her indoor cat, Sky, fell through the window screen and decided to stay outside. She knew of all his outdoor hiding places: under the neighbor's porch, in the flower bed of geraniums, and under her own home. It was going on two months now, and although Sky ate the food Georgiane left for him on the porch, and even came by to rub noses with his feline sisters through the glass door, he would not come inside. When the temperatures began to drop to fifteen degrees, Georgiane called me for help. She didn't think that Sky knew how to get back in the house.

When I asked Sky why he wasn't coming home, I felt anxiety. He said he wasn't heard. He wanted to explore parts of himself that he hadn't explored. This is how I interpreted Sky's thoughts about not being heard. "Georgiane needs to explore parts of herself. Those parts that have been forgotten. She has a heavy heart. I have tried to tell her. She doesn't speak up for herself. She is not accepting the way things are. The way things turned out. She keeps beating her head against the same wall. She doesn't stop. She doesn't see. Too much work. She takes care of everyone except herself. Her heart is broken. Too many times. I want her to look at herself. Look at me! I threw it all away. I am a free spirit. She doesn't see this. She just wants me back. I'll come back when I'm ready."

I told Sky that this wasn't entirely true. Georgiane did respect and honor his decision. So much, that she was willing to let him come and go as he pleased. But now, he really needed to return. I explained that if the snow fell and piled up, it would be harder for him to find food, and it would be extremely cold. I mentally showed him how to get inside his home.

Sky knew his person well. Georgiane told me about the trauma in her life: leaving her husband, working sixty to eighty hours a week to support her son through college, becoming sick, and then losing her home in a fire and having to move into a hotel room with her son and her six animals, before moving into the condo. She especially missed her paint brushes. Her paint-stained brushes with bristles worn to stumps had once held the faint scent of sweet turpentine and personal freedom. I understood the attachment. I also couldn't part with my gloriously retired oil paint brushes, which haven't been used in twenty-one years. Georgiane knew she had to paint again. She had to start over. She had to somehow cut her hours back at work and speak to her son. She hadn't wanted to burden him, but now she felt ready to speak her mind. She also needed to forgive her husband, to release resentments and heal her broken heart.

"I used to be a free spirit," Georgiane told me. "I've forgotten."

Georgiane made some clear-cut decisions in her life, and waited for Sky to return.

You Don't See Me

Darla was pissed off. I fed the cat when Nate and Sharon traveled. They said Darla was used to the routine, because they had been traveling for years. But every time Sharon and Nate left, Darla greeted me with growls, hisses and claw bats. When I left for work, she followed me, screamed at my ankles and bit them hard. I made sure she knew when Nate and Sharon were returning, but it did no good. Every time they left, Darla reacted the same way. After a few days, she would relax and go back to normal. She slept all day on my bed and had no desire to go outside. I realized that Darla's tough, snarly facade masked a longing for affection and love.

However, when Sharon and Nate were home, Darla was nowhere to be seen. Sharon wanted to know why Darla was never home. I found Darla's heart center was shut down. She was lonely, and she did not feel loved or special. If you didn't feel welcomed or noticed, you would leave too.

I told Sharon to work on talking to Darla as a family member. I suggested she tell her cat what was going on in the home, how busy her schedule was with the children, and how happy she was to have Darla around. Of course, Sharon had to mean it. Words are empty to an animal if your intentions are not from the heart. Fortunately, Sharon did truly love her cat.

I told Sharon that, instead of topping off the cat's dry food bowl with more of the same, she could make an effort and feed Darla twice a day—even call her in for a surprise treat. Can you imagine how boring it would be to have a bowl of dry, stale cereal on your table to eat morning, noon and night? Yet we dish this out to our animals for our own convenience.

Animals, especially cats, require a variety of protein in their diet. Cats are creatures of habit, and if they are exposed to only one type of food—especially if it is a cheaper one filled with food additives and chemicals—chances are, this is all they will accept. It is up to you to slowly break them from the addictive taste trap and introduce healthier foods that are not processed. It is the same as breaking a child's habit of the high they are accustomed to feeling from eating potato chips, sugar and cooked animal flesh.[7] Getting kids to eat steamed broccoli can take a while.

Dry food is also the worst food to feed cats.[8] It absorbs the water in their bodies, dehydrating them and stressing the kidneys. Cats are desert animals and do not normally drink much water. If they do, they have a problem.

Now that Sharon understood how much Darla hated being left home alone, she agreed to find a sitter for long trips. I told Darla that her humans were trying their best, and that she needed to make an effort as well. Afterwards, I didn't see Darla around for quite some time. I worried that something had happened to her. When I asked, Sharon told me Darla was spending more time in the house with the family.

The truth is, cats need you just as much as dogs do. They are not independent. Felines bond with their humans just as much as any other animal. Most cats survive just fine outdoors, but they prefer a warm bed and a human body to cozy up to.

Louise, one of my feral felines, comes indoors to take her afternoon nap.[9] My other feral, Smokey, who had lived an outdoor life for twelve

---

[7]   Yogi Bhajan, PhD, Master of Kundalini Yoga, says that flesh instantly raises serotonin levels, giving one a high.

[8]   You can read about the benefits of a raw meat diet for cats and dogs, and see recipes on this website: www.CharlesLoops.com. Be sure to add supplements such as: calcium, fish oil, a multivitamin. For cats, add taurine. Digestive enzymes are also beneficial for both a natural or processed food diet. Grapefruit seed extract is a natural parasite and worm expeller, if you have concerns about parasites. www.danielleldon.net

[9]   After two of my cats were killed by cars, and one disappeared, I assembled a six hundred forty-square-foot, open-ceiling enclosure made of netting, curved at the top to prevent them from jumping out. www.kittyfence.com

years and gave birth to her children in a chimney, rarely leaves the house. I have rescued both domestic and feral[10] cats, both of whom have had their fill of the streets. While every animal has individual preferences, all animals need more than food and water. They need companionship and love and to know that their lives matter.

---

[10] Feral cats are the offspring of domestic cats who have not been socialized (touched by humans).

CHAPTER 9

WHEN THE ISSUE IS THEIRS,
YOU'RE OFF THE HOOK—BUT
YOU STILL NEED TO LISTEN

*...Animals' emotions are raw, unfiltered, and uncontrolled.
Their joy is the purest and most contagious of joys and
their grief the deepest and most devastating...*

Marc Bekoff,
The Emotional Lives of Animals

Not every situation is a mirror of you. Animals have their own karma to work through and their own spiritual paths to follow. Yet again, in their attempt to let you know that something is wrong with them physically or emotionally, they will sometimes act out aggressively, eliminate inappropriately, bark, cry, or display odd behavior. Living with animals is a game of charades. Understand that they are only trying to communicate.

When I found small puddles and spots of blood in random places throughout the house, I knew someone was asking for help. I didn't know who, since I had seven cats at the time. I closed my eyes and mentally asked whoever needed help to please come and show me now.

Ertha jumped right on the bed with me, squatted, and pushed out a drop of blood. She had a urinary tract infection. Animals are smart. Ertha knew if she went to the litter box, I would have never noticed the blood.

Take Me Out!

Alison called me again when her cat Savanna was peeing on the kitchen floor, in the kitchen sink and on the couches. Alison had already taken the cat to the vet, who ruled out UTI (urinary tract infection).

Since Savanna was not targeting her person's clothes, bed or bedroom, I knew this wasn't something directly related to her person, as it was before when Savanna was upset over Alison's divorce. At this time, Alison was still married, so I assumed there was probably discord in the house, perhaps arguing between her and her husband. I was wrong. Right away, Savanna told me, "I liked the other place better," and flashed me an image of an outdoor courtyard. She wanted to know why she could no longer go out. I had no idea that Alison had moved. Sure enough, the former apartment had a courtyard where Savanna was allowed out a few hours a day. The present apartment had nothing similar. I suggested Alison put a harness on Savanna and take her outside. She did. Savanna was happy again and stopped urinating outside the box.

Lucia and Her Litter Box

Cats are quite meticulous creatures, and they do not like their litter boxes dirty. They also have their preferences. One cat told me she did not use her litter box because she did not like the way it was positioned, half under a chair.

Lucia, a two-year-old indoor cat, told me her litter made her sick. Her person, Janet, doubted this. This was the only litter Lucia had ever known, and she had used it since kitten-hood. Convincing Janet she had nothing to lose, I suggested changing the fine-grain, clumping type of litter to a heavier, textured pellet shaped litter. Lucia loved the new litter and never soiled the carpets again.

Big Boy And Joe

Every year, I donate my services to the Stray Cat Alliance, a rescue organization that spays and neuters thousands of feral cats in the lower income areas of Los Angeles. At their gala fundraisers, I give free consultations. One year, a tall, large man named Joe asked me why his cat, Big Boy, continually ran away from him. He was two years old and had been running since birth.

Immediately, Big Boy said, "I'm afraid he's going to fall on me." I explained to Joe's cat that humans walk vertically, and although we do trip and fall once in a great while, the chances were that we would not. I told him that if Joe did fall, he would have plenty of time to move out of the way. I never heard back from Joe until I saw him the following year at the same event. He was ecstatic. He told me that when he returned home from the fundraiser one year earlier, Big Boy did not run from him—and he never ran from him again.

A Chosen Path

I was volunteering my services at an outdoor animal adoption event when I met Parsley, a medium-sized dog with long, sienna-colored fur. Maureen showed him in competitions, although lately, Parsley was not performing well. He knew his routine and did well in rehearsals, but when the competitions came around, Parsley refused to participate.

I did not feel that Parsley was opposed to being a show dog. I sensed that there was something else he would rather be doing, but I had no idea what that was. When I asked Parsley, I received no answer. Intuitively I sent healing energy to her dog and dropped all expectations.

As I was running energy, tiny orange lights bounced all over Parsley's body, and the dog smiled. The words "healer dog" came into my mind. Thrilled, I spilled it to Maureen: "Parsley is a healer dog!" Maureen's jaw dropped. When she had rescued Parsley as a puppy, she had thought of using him as a therapy dog. Now she knew that being a show dog was the wrong profession for her dog. Parsley's job was to help people, and he knew it.

Had Maureen really thought of Parsley being a therapy dog when he arrived as a puppy? Or had Parsley chosen this for himself, and Maureen had picked up on his thoughts?

Our animals do have a purpose in life. And their purpose is not to lie around all day to sleep and eat, or to live in the back yard or be told to shut up or shooed away. One animal communicator's dog barked nonstop whenever anyone arrived. Hosting a workshop at her house meant that her dog barked when each participant drove up or entered the home. We could barely hear each other speak over the dog's ear-piercing monologue. The communicator never told her dog to stop barking and never put him alone in another room or discouraged him from barking in any way. She knew this was his job: greeting all the guests. And he did his job well.

All animals need a job. Not all will have professions like Parsley. Jobs may range from getting the paper, protecting the house, providing companionship to another animal, waking their humans up in the morning, chasing other animals out of the yard, or barking at the mail person. Be attentive. Figure out what your animal's job is or assign them one. Having a purpose builds an animal's self-esteem and sense of importance. Animals are family members and should never be expected to live by our rigid human standards.

Looking For A Job?

Flora was a female cat who was aggressive toward her other two feline companions. Tara called me to iron things out. She told me that Flora attacked the others, and she wasn't playing. Immediately after the session all three cats sat peacefully in the living room together— for the first time. From that day forward Flora left the other two cats alone. Tara also noticed that the next day, and for the days thereafter, Flora had incorporated a new routine into her life. She sat on the front porch and seemed to be guarding the house, chasing other cats out of the yard and looking quite content and proud. Tara now called her the Guard Kitty. During our session I had told Flora that instead of beating up her housemates, she needed to protect them, and to protect the whole house as well. My intention was to give Flora a purpose in the household. It must have sounded like a good idea to Flora, for it became her new job.

Eight years later Tara called when she had not seen her Guard Kitty all day. Staying away was not Flora's routine, and Tara feared that something had happened to her. When I connected with Flora I got very little description of her surroundings. What I did describe to Tara seemed to fit the description of her neighbor's home to the North. Flora had sent me an image of a cowboy hat and a shovel, so Tara checked the shed with the cowboy hat and all the sheds on her neighbor's property. I hoped she was trapped somewhere and that someone would open their garage doors and send her home. But Flora was not turning up.

Next I did a body scan. I felt a sharp pain in my head and neck area. I feared Flora was injured. Then I did a Remote Viewing for Flora, and I experienced a bi-lo,[11] something that I had never experienced before.

Since I wasn't seeing much of anything as I mind-traveled to the target site, I set an intention by mentally stating, "Show me what happened to Flora." Then I continued to lay relaxed and comfortable under a blanket, with earplugs, blindfold and a "pink noise" recording to help me access a deep, meditative, Theta brainwave state, and to also block out all sensory distractions. About three minutes went by when I felt as if I were suffocating. I started coughing and choking and could not breathe. I gasped for air and began heaving with the breath, almost hyperventilating. I felt an almost intolerable burning, paralyzing ache through my right thigh, and my heart pounded in terror. I stopped the Viewing.

I knew without a doubt that Flora was no longer alive in her physical body, and I had to tell Tara. Delivering this information to people is the hardest thing to do. And although I don't usually tell someone that I think their animal may be dead (because most people cannot handle this information, and because there is no way to ever be one hundred percent certain if an animal is in or out of the body), I was certain Flora had gotten attacked by a predator. I wasn't sure of the species, but I knew the predator was brown and smaller than a coyote. I knew Flora wouldn't be coming home. Both Tara and I hoped that my findings were wrong. She continued her search for her

---

[11] A bi-lo, or bi-location, is a phenomenon where the Viewer experiences physical sensations that indicate what is happening in the target site.

Guard Kitty, but Flora was never found. Much later, a bobcat was sighted roaming the neighborhood.

A Horse's Dream

The most important thing I stress to beginners in my own workshops is to trust every bit of information they get. I tell students to pay attention to the feelings in their body and to every thought, smell, and sound that enters their mind, and not to discount anything. Images are not only packed with information, but they can be delivered symbolically or in metaphor—the same way our subconscious minds deliver messages to us in dreams. When we receive symbolic information in dreams, we are forced to dig deeper into ourselves. When we receive this sort of information while talking to an animal, we need to ask the animal to clarify.

Dusty, a brown mare, was angry, extremely depressed and barely eating. She would not allow anyone near her. No one knew what to do. As I sat in silence, ready to receive answers from Dusty, an old friend came to mind, and I had no idea why. My friend, Chrono, had been a singer in an experimental fusion band in Los Angeles. Gradually, he had lost his ability to walk. Before long, he could no longer talk. He had several tests and saw numerous allopathic and holistic doctors, all of whom were stumped. Chrono lived the rest of his life in silence bound to a wheelchair until he died in his early forties.

I wondered what the correlation was between my friend and this depressed horse when these words resounded in my mind. *Chrono was not able to live out his creative dreams.* When I feel a wrench in the solar plexus, the gut, sometimes accompanied by goosebumps, I know I have hit the truth. Something had happened which deeply disturbed Dusty. What had robbed this mare of her creative dreams?

What were her dreams? Dusty conveyed that she had never been given the opportunity to have offspring. She had wanted to be a mother.

Animals want families as much as humans do. It saddens me that we have to spay and neuter our domestic dogs and cats without their consent. However, in Los Angeles and most other large cities, spaying and neutering is the humane method of population control. Otherwise, too many unwanted animals are created, and many are killed in the shelters—thousands of dogs and cats a year in Los Angeles, and millions nationwide. Our domestic animal over-population is such a huge problem that Los Angeles finally passed a mandatory spay and neuter ordinance. The goal was to have fewer animals wind up abandoned, surrendered at the pound, or starved or poisoned on the streets. Not allowing our animals to reproduce (and not having to find the babies homes) also gives animals already impounded a greater chance of being adopted. Spaying and neutering also reduces the chances of our animals roaming and getting into fights, being hit by cars, or winding up in the wrong hands.

Beatrice's Pregnancy

Beatrice was not herself. The dog was acting strangely, Lyn said. Beatrice had taken her toys and placed them together on the bed. She sat on them and growled if anyone, including Lyn, came too close. Lyn thought her dog Beatrice was having a pseudo pregnancy.

I went to see the gentle Golden Retriever. Extreme sadness struck me when I saw the longing in sweet Beatrice's eyes. She told me she wanted to have babies. Beatrice was not spayed, although Lyn had no intentions of letting her have puppies. I told the dog I was so sorry and that I understood her desire. I explained why the option of offspring was out of the question. I told Beatrice about the laws in the city and all the animals who were unwanted and killed because there were not enough homes, explaining that this was the reason Lyn could not let her have children.

I smell skepticism. Do animals understand all this, you ask? Animals understand more than we realize. Perhaps they do not understand what a law is, but they can interpret and understand the pictures and concepts behind the words.

That evening, Beatrice took her toys off the bed and was back to being herself. I did not ask her to remove her toys. She did that of her own choosing. Having the forgivable, accepting-what-is attitude that animals have, she let go.

Almost A Landscape Of Miracles

Janko approached Penny for help, as feral cats often do when they are sick. He was dying when he found Penny, and he never fully recovered. Permanently disabled, Janko could not see or hear well. His head shook and slanted to one side. Penny hand fed him for the two years he was with her until the day she called me, heartbroken. Janko had ducked outside two days after Thanksgiving and had not returned. She had no idea how he could possibly survive out there on his own.

Janko chose to stay directly across the street, despite my efforts to persuade him to return. After a while, he disappeared from that neighbor's house, and in mid-January, Penny spotted the cat in the backyard of a couple who rescued cats. It turns out that Janko had shown up there sometime in December, and the couple had fed him, given him antibiotics in his food, and provided him with a relatively safe and comfortable place to live outside. Janko found a girlfriend and started to look healthy and robust. Penny felt that she had entered a magical realm—in her words, a landscape of miracles—when she found him.

Janko grew more feral and would not allow anyone to pick him up, nor would he go into the humane trap. Penny did get to hold him for a few seconds one day until he squirmed out of her arms. She visited every day just to watch him and talk to him, although she knew that Janko had no intentions of ever returning on his own.

Then Janko disappeared from the couple's home in late April and was never seen again. Seven months later, I spoke to Penny. "Janko got to die with his boots on, as the cat he wanted to be, and I must be OK with that and live my life," Penny told me. "I have had many losses recently. My mother passed, and I have lost count of the number of my cats who have died from various causes, along with two dogs. The possibility of finding Janko and bringing him home was the thing that sustained me. To know that I was given the chance and lost it is really painful."

It is hard to accept that sometimes our animals do not wish to return. Sometimes animals will make their home with another human, either purposely or against their will. They may need to move on to help someone else. In the larger picture, animals have their own agendas, spiritual agreements, and life work. In Janko's case, he returned to his feral roots. Despite his handicap, he chose to live as a free cat.

Where's My Mother?

Neither Bianca nor her husband could get near Ziti, the new donkey they had purchased a few short months earlier. Ziti kicked, cornered, bit and attacked anyone who got close. At feeding time, Bianca's husband thought he could bond with the donkey, but Ziti charged and would not accept her food. Her aggressive behavior was unpredictable. Bianca had to drop her expectations of training Ziti to be a therapy animal for children. But she wanted to know why Ziti was so angry and if she would prefer to return to the farm where she was purchased.

My eyes welled up in tears when I tuned-in to Ziti. Immediately I felt extreme sadness and grief. I asked Ziti if she wanted to talk to me. She said she didn't have much to say. I asked Ziti why she was angry, and I heard, "Where is my mother?"

I told her I did not know, but that I would find out. I asked her what the farm was like and if she wanted to go back. Ziti showed me what looked like an unkempt, crowded place where she had spent most of her time in the pasture, away from humans. She did not want to go back. I sensed that the farm was like a puppy mill. Then she said, "They took my mother away." I asked her if her mother was living on the farm with her. "Yes, but now I don't see her."

Why was she angry? Again I heard one sentence: "I want to know where my mother is." I probed as much as I could. I asked Ziti if she liked Bianca and her husband, if she liked her food and her new home. I asked her a slew of other questions as well. I heard nothing except, "What happened to my mother?"

I turned to Bianca. "Do you know anything about Ziti's mother?"

The question knocked Bianca cold. Ziti had come from a farm that bred and sold ponies and donkeys for profit. Ziti had never known her biological mom, but had bonded from birth with a surrogate mother—a white goat with a pink nose, named Rotelli. Rotelli was all Ziti knew, and they were so attached that the owners of the farm told Bianca that she could not buy Ziti without taking Rotelli. They went together, or not at all. So Bianca had brought them both to her home in Upstate New York.

Soon, Bianca realized she could not hold Ziti's attention long enough to train her for therapy work. Enamored with Rotelli, Ziti ignored Bianca and every human. The days passed. Friends came up with the perfect solution. Get rid of Rotelli. Then Ziti will give Bianca her undivided attention. Or so they thought.

Ziti deeply mourned the absence of her mother, friend, and lifelong companion. Now Bianca searched frantically, tracking the people who were supposed to know of Rotelli's whereabouts. She did all she could to retrieve the goat, even after she was told by a ranch hand that Rotelli had been eaten by a coyote. Certain this was not so, she continued calling everyone she could.

Rotelli was never located. Bianca did the next best thing. She found a kind woman living on a ranch with sheep, goats, horses and two donkeys, who was willing to take Ziti, and Bianca let her go. Bianca's heart was in the right place. She provided the next best home for Ziti.

Although there is often no simple solution, there is a common mistaken assumption that "others out there" will fill an animal's void. Animals have special friends and loved ones, and they grieve their losses, just as we do. If we can remember or realize that animals are no different from us, it will be easier to feel what they feel. How do we feel when we lose a loved one? Do we bond as readily with others of our kind? In the soup of humans who surround us, can we find a replacement and share the same intimacy that we had before? These things take time. Some of us never move on. Even when we do, there remains a place in our hearts for the one who is no longer with us.

Animals are gravely misunderstood and underestimated. A newscaster had excitedly reported that a fisherman hauled in a short-raker rockfish, a species that is said to live two hundred years. Much to everyone's disappointment, the rockfish was possibly sixty-four, at most ninety-five. It could not be released back to sea, since once brought up from those depths its bladder fills with air, and it cannot survive. It was destroyed for no reason, this fish who was not yet middle aged, while everyone celebrated the biggest catch in history. Was I the only one who cried?

Fish, no matter what size, are highly intelligent. They have highly developed nervous systems like ours, and they feel pain. They do not choose to swim alone in small circles above colored stones in decorative bowls. They have families and friends like any other living being. When I visit my friend Michael, his fish recognize me and rush to the front of the tank wagging their tails. Michael has a large tank with an assortment of plants, tunnels, and hiding places which he rearranges every few months so his fish companions won't be bored.

Do we view animals as sentient beings and truly feel how they feel? If we would not want to see our animal companions stabbed in the roof of their mouths by a needle-sharp hook, then hauled through the air to be drowned in a tub, why would we even think of going fishing?

Do we have the right to take another being's life? I struggled with myself, since I took my own cat's life when she clearly was not ready.

Confessions of An Animal Communicator

How did Ertha know something was wrong with her blood? And why didn't I hear her desperate pleas for help? I had in the past. I was annoyed with my cat. Ertha pooped in the two spots in my house that I most frequented: the entrance of the bathroom and closet. Wrapped up in my summer job, teaching art to children, I thought she was upset that I wasn't home.

I held her feces to her face one day as if she had committed a heinous crime as I scowled, "WHY are you doing this?" Ertha stood up, embarrassed in her bed. Her eyes lowered as she hung her head. She was a good kitty who looked after me like a mother and had never done anything she considered wrong. My first and only female cat, a multicolored muted Tortie, Ertha had brought harmony into my house of battling boys. She even hung from Bootsie's neck to engage the grouchy feral in play.

She was two months old when I had rescued her in a parking lot on Skid Row, where the homeless sleep in cardboard beds in the streets of downtown Los Angeles. It was the exact date that Neostradomous had predicted the big earthquake that might hit Los Angeles. I had just finished teaching an art class to homeless women at the Downtown Women's Center, and was trudging through the sprawling lot to my car. I remembered the prediction and thought, *what will happen today that will shake my world?* Suddenly Ertha drew me to her with her guttural screams for help. Assuming the cry was from one of the sea gulls, I scanned the parking lot and saw the flock of birds to the far west of the lot. But the squawks continued to pull my attention toward the opposite direction. Finally I spotted a little lump, spread eagle on the asphalt. As I got closer and stood over the kitten, she raised her head to face me and wailed again and again pleading from the heart. I took her home in a grocery bag. Now she was ten years old.

I apologized for humiliating her, for not being home and for keeping her bored inside. I never asked her what was wrong. She continued to defecate on the floor. Then one night, she slept at my side—something she rarely did if the boys were sprawled around me. That evening in my dream, she stood there, then walked away leaving behind a puddle of blood.

Was she telling me she was losing her life force? The possibility of her dying was unthinkable. My Dad had recently died, weeks before his ninetieth birthday, and I was still grieving Bubby, who had whittled away from kidney failure and died two months after my Father. I could not bear to lose Ertha now, or ever.

She had a ravenous appetite and was even a few pounds overweight. She was the healthiest of all. She ate so much, in fact, that I reduced her portions. I convinced myself that the dream was just a dream.

I sleepwalked in a padded mind of preoccupation as Ertha slept more and grew thin. Hijacked by the projects I would teach tomorrow, I remained blind to her attempts to alert me that she needed help.

The day she stopped eating, I took her to the vet.

As Ertha had indicated, there was something indeed wrong with her blood. Her sugar levels were soaring, her ketones (dangerous acid buildup) were high, and she tested positive for the Feline Leukemia virus—even though she had tested negative as a kitten. The vet suspected diabetes. Fearing that she might go into a coma, I asked if she could stay the night for surveillance. The doctor said no. She reassured me that Ertha would be fine, saying that high blood sugar levels don't cause comas as low sugar levels do. She asked me to expect a call from her promptly at 8:30 a.m. with the blood test results.

The phone never rang the next morning. I called the hospital three times, but the doctor was too busy to talk to me. Finally, I listened to my hunches in art class that morning and flew home on break to find Ertha immobile by her water bowl. She could not pick up her head. I told her we were going back to the vet and asked if she would be all right. "Yes, I'll pull through," I heard.

The receptionist at the Animal Hospital told me not to come until I spoke to the doctor, since nothing could be done until all of her test results returned. I took her in anyway.

I never heard from the doctor that morning, that afternoon, or that evening. Not before, during, or even after Ertha's death. In fact, no one called me from the hospital, so I assumed Ertha had pulled through just fine. I didn't know until I arrived ten hours later to take her home that I would be taking Ertha's torpid body to the Emergency Animal Clinic instead.

It was a cold, sterile clinic, where an abrupt receptionist kept me waiting another forty minutes in the lobby with my feeble cat. Then someone finally swept Ertha away to the examination room, as I waited in a small cell to speak to the doctor. He presented the downside of her condition and an unpromising recovery. He emphasized a costly and laborious intervention on top of his grim prognosis, and suggested euthanasia. My mind circled in confusion. The doctor waited for an answer—the answer that would save or end Ertha's life. Either way, it seemed, would be fine with him. He stood there expressionless, as though I were choosing between a pair of shoes. I excused myself, more than once, to sit in my car. I thought that sitting in the dark, deserted lot might open the space I needed for clarity. I sat in my old jeep, which now felt like the only friend I had. I begged for guidance, searched through my contact list for someone to call and hoped for some sort of sign. I waited for a divine spark to illuminate the muddle. But my mind spun faster, and my focus grew dimmer, while Ertha grew weaker with every procrastinating minute. I went back inside and asked to see her again. I asked her what she wanted me to do, but the torrent of my emotions buried Ertha's whispers, and I still had no answers for the doctor, or myself. After three hours of indecision at the Emergency Clinic, I came to a decision.

Twice Ertha had found an ounce of strength to raise her head, turn and face me. First, when she sensed my partner Michael entering the building, and again just before the doctor entered the room with the syringe in his coat pocket. She didn't appear "obtunded" then, as the doctor had indicated, and I almost changed my mind. I don't know why I didn't. Several Skid Row screams bellowed through the room before she flopped back down in exhaustion. The vet inserted the needle and all life left her body. I had given consent, despite the twisted feelings of indecision in my gut—a clear no.

I will never know whether Ertha was yelling goodbye or begging me to help her live. The decision I made that evening has kept me wondering if Ertha would have pulled through as she had said she would. I didn't give her a fighting chance.

When we do not listen, we do not hear. When our emotions sabotage us, our minds are scattered and not clear. We can't tune in to our inner guidance, and we are not open to receive. We decide in doubt, confusion, and interference instead of clear knowing and open channels. When we take things into our own hands and forget to step out of the way to allow natural healing, and to trust karma and divine decisions to unfold, we may regret our actions for a lifetime.

Was it Ertha's time to go? Did the universe line things up for it to happen? If we are all actors on the stage, playing our parts to orchestrate and present our life lessons to ourselves and others, then I was not the only one with my head in the mud. Let's look at the line-up: There was the vet who did not take immediate action and hospitalize Ertha, and who was too busy to look at her test results that next morning. There were the technicians who kept Ertha waiting for an hour in the lobby when I had rushed her in for emergency care. And other technicians who did not start treatment until three hours after she was brought in, and then administered three injections of insulin on an empty stomach, instead of inserting a feeding tube, which sent Ertha's sugar levels flying off the charts.

There was the Emergency Clinic vet who was quick to wash his hands of it all by pushing euthanasia, diagnosing her white gums and lips as a symptom of liver damage when white gums indicate a diabetic shock. Had we all played out our "mistakes"? Was I simply an idiot who made wrong choices, or was I an intuitive who made the most compassionate choice for another who was suffering? I had dropped the blame and the "if onlys"—except for self-blame. I, out of everyone, should have heard her.

Months later, I considered our soul contracts with one another. Although it did not assuage my grief at all, I wondered if this tragedy was part of the soul contract that I had worked out with Ertha—and if so, what were the blessings and lessons I was to learn from her passing? What were her lessons? I felt nothing but despair and self-hatred, and the intolerable regret that haunts one forever.

Blessings From Ertha

Lessons? The tragedy humbled me. I was no longer as quick to judge others, which is something I work on every day. It's easy to put up a wall and hate others for their actions. It has been especially hard for me not to judge others who hurt animals. Yet at the time, if I had been less self-centered and more present, I would have known Ertha was asking for help. If I'd had the consciousness then that I have now, I would not have done what I now regret. If I had been present with Ertha, I might have been guided to take the right actions.

When we don't learn what we need to learn, we are presented with similar scenarios until we do. And so it is. All of us are here to evolve, learn life lessons, and love unconditionally—in step and in congruence with the bigger picture. Our animals are here to open our hearts. If we did not open to our suffering, how would we ever know joy and feel compassion?

With all my babbling about enlightenment, it took me nearly three years to forgive myself and all those involved. Forgiving does not mean condoning. It means creating an opening for oneself to heal. For when we hold hard our resentments, we close down, and the tunnel only gets darker.

Two years after Ertha's death I attended my second silent retreat in the desert. During a Tibetan Buddhist practice on forgiveness, something big welled up inside and burst like a dam. I forgave everyone who I felt hurt me. I opened to all the unconscious and conscious acts of violence that we do to ourselves and each other out of fear and through our delusion of separateness. For the first time I felt a softening within, instead of hard walled anger and hatred. I forgave myself for all my unkind words, thoughts and actions that have caused harm to others. I forgave myself for hurting those I loved out of selfishness, insensitivity and fear.

I felt love for anyone who had ever hurt, humiliated, or shamed me, knowing that they did what they did from ignorance and pain. I saw that everyone in my life was a mirror, throwing me back to myself. So I thanked those teachers who presented pain in my path for me to work through at my own pace.

It was especially difficult forgiving myself, the animal communicator who claimed to listen to animals, but when I forgave myself for killing Ertha, I felt the entire universe sweep through me. I sobbed for weeks, not from sadness, but from being deeply touched, sincerely humbled and grateful to be here. To have known her. To have finally realized that I did what I did because I loved her, and because I was small and scared.

As my heart opened, I felt embraced and forgiven. I cried when others cried, when the rain fell, and especially when the wind blew and reminded me I was here, alive, and not alone. I swelled with tears when I woke in the morning or as I drove down the street. I wept when I thought of Ertha. I wept at the memory of my youth and the death of my mother, remembering it all from the eyes of a little girl. I wept for all the times I didn't weep. And I realized that I hadn't cried in years, and that finally, I had truly surrendered to the process of grieving.

I wept at everything I saw. I felt deep gratitude and awe for my life and all life. I wept for all my losses, and for the losses of others, and for the eternal bond we share with one another through the breadth of our human condition—our suffering and joy. Blessings are bittersweet, no matter who delivers them or how they are delivered.

The stab is still sharp when I think of my pale tan and gray girl with her assorted stripes and spots, who wailed in a voice like Eartha Kitt, and who will wail in my heart forever. Forgiving myself didn't take the pain away, and it didn't bring Ertha back. But it allowed me to meet the confusion and darkness that prevailed in my mind that night with some light and understanding. And this understanding has helped me to soften toward others who have also said or done things out of confusion and darkness. I felt sprinkled with gentleness instead of weighed down with self-hatred and harsh judgement, at least for a while. Forgiving myself has become a process that remains first on my daily to-do list.

Perhaps this is why I live with animals. They are professors in the higher schools of unconditional love and forgiveness. Forgiveness eventually blossoms into compassion. Compassion grows into unconditional love. Loving ourselves unconditionally, as our animals love us, becomes the first step in the right direction. My animals are continual reminders that unconditional love may be the ultimate crawl to enlightenment.

Ertha, a loner like me, took a liking to Yudi. She was his consort. Yudi let out his special yowl for her, and she ran to him, even from a sound sleep. They tangled together as Yudi faux-mated and bit her neck. She loved him. Had she been grief-stricken when he died? She would have nothing to do with any of the other males. Not even O'Henry, who continually tried to entice her into play. Had she lost the sweetness in life? No longer allowed outdoors when I moved, she stared at the trees everyday from her window seat.

I wondered why Ertha manifested diabetes in her body, and why I chose not to see it. I wondered why I chose to take life away from her instead of giving her a chance to fight. I will always wonder why confusion created such a dense barrier between myself and my intuition that night. I finally realized that Yudi had come back as a cat to open my heart, but Ertha was the one who succeeded.

CHAPTER 10

FIVE WAYS TO LISTEN TO ANIMALS

You will see how simple life is.
As you learn not-knowing,
your heart will find its way home.
The Second Book of The Tao, Verse 59
Translated by Stephen Mitchell

A nimal communication is not only possible, it is the groundwork that makes communication with all life possible. Anyone can learn to do this. When you do, your reality will never be quite the same again. If you are human, you already have the abilities. You just need to stir in five important ingredients before you begin.

Here are some things to check in yourself if you want to deepen your relationship with your animal companions, to prepare yourself to listen and be open to receive.

1. Slow The Chatter In Your Mind

If you have five channels going at once, your animals will only pick up your static and confusion. Someone once said to me, "What are you talking about? I don't have any chatter in my mind." Try this experiment if you do not think you are bombarded with thought talk.

Sit down, settle in, and focus on your breathing. Become aware of your inhalation and exhalation. Keep your attention on your breath as you count mentally from one to ten. Inhale, exhale, one. Inhale, exhale, two, etc. Chances are, you will not be able to count past five before your mind will have wandered and your awareness will have fallen off your breath. When this happens, grab the reigns, get back on, and ride the breath again.

Thought is the nature of the mind. You cannot stop thinking, but you can become aware that you're thinking. Eventually, through breath awareness, you can ride your thoughts. You can notice a thought enter your mind and allow it to be there without identifying with it, without being swept up into it and becoming it. In other words, you can choose *not* to think your thoughts and remain present with your breath instead. Eventually, you will notice your thoughts rise and fall, and then gently disappear like clouds in the sky. You will see you are not your thoughts.

Allowing thoughts to pass is difficult, because our ego wants to hold on and distract us. It prefers to take us on a roller coaster winding to the past, thrusting to the future or suspending us in fantasy. Our attention is constantly sideswiped by the external world as our minds engage us in inner dialogue and mental activity. The ego does not want to disappear. But when it does, we find ourselves merged within a peaceful, expanded state of consciousness. The present moment, as subtle as the still point between breaths, is where we tap into the Quantum Field, Source Energy, the Matrix Field or God. It's also where we can tap into the thoughts and feelings of our animals.

Little did I know that the years I spent painting, drawing and meditating would set the foundation for the work I do today. I have learned to sit for long periods in silence and focused attention, listening and responding to the moment and not allowing my mind to float away with thoughts. Although I'm no longer engaged in the visual arts, meditation needs to be practiced daily or my mind can easily return to its roller coaster nature again.

Children in my art classes were often out of control, spinning, scooting around the room, or rocking. (They usually ate donuts for breakfast and processed foods for lunch.) I sat them in a circle for meditation every day. In the midst of loud chatter and distraction, I would strike the small brass bowl, used in Buddhist meditation. Its melodic, lingering resonance drifted through the room commanding their attention, while they sat still listening to the sound taper into silence. All talking ceased, and each child in the class, gong-struck in stillness, folded their hands in prayer pose. I didn't ask them to. The sound of the gong was enough to bring them inward into the present. Any sound, smell, or taste can do the same thing and strike through our internal chatter. We "wake-up" in intervals like this throughout our life, but then we slip back into our busy minds. When we learn to consciously control our breath, we can master our thoughts. Staying awake takes practice.

At another school, I met Ian, a seven-year-old on prescription drugs. Ian walked in circles grumbling to himself and striking the air. His teacher said he did this often, and she handled it by ignoring him. I took him aside, sat him down, and asked him to look up at the sky.

"Do you see the vastness of the sky, Ian? How smooth and peaceful it is?"

Gong-struck by the sky, Ian looked up and nodded. For a few minutes, we both stared at the still, blue space.

"It goes on forever, Ian. It's so big. Your mind is like the sky," I told him. "It's vast and smooth. You don't have to listen or be bothered by those thoughts in your head. Your thoughts are just like clouds in the sky. They come and go. You can let them pass. When you feel scared, Ian, just remember to look at the sky. Expand out. You are the sky, not your thoughts." I asked Ian to bring his attention to the tip of his nostrils and feel his breath enter and leave, to relax his mind and ground him in his body.

The boy immediately calmed down and went back to the classroom. I hoped that his physicians did this sort of thing with him and did not just pump him up with more Ritalin.

Our animals want us to look at the sky. When we slow our busy minds to the wavelength of our animals' minds, we are in a powerful place. When martial artists are about to break a slab of concrete, their minds do not wander off to what needs to be done next. Nor will you ever see a Zen monk eating dinner while watching TV. Remember, we cannot be here if we are somewhere else. We cannot hear unless we listen. And to listen requires our complete presence.

2. Believe It Is Possible

Once upon a time, it was believed that the world was flat. When we believe that the world is composed of, or limited to, that which we perceive through our five senses, then our world still remains somewhat flat. Believe that you are more than blood and bones. You are energy. All of us are spiritual beings in an assortment of physical bodies.

If you are skeptical or doubt you can communicate with animals— or if you do not believe talking to animals is possible for anyone— you may block information from flowing in. This is one reason I only work with people who contact me requesting my help. These people are open to possibilities. Otherwise, with channels closed or hindered by one's skepticism, the dialogue with the animal may not flow as freely. Our thoughts become cemented beliefs that color our perceptions and form our reality.

It's natural to doubt our abilities. It took years for me to believe in myself. The most convincing validations have come from wild animals, those with whom I had absolutely no egotistical expectations with or pressure to "be right."

I connected with unseen coyotes at Griffith Park in Los Angeles, knowing they were lurking somewhere beyond the woodsy horizon. I asked if they could hear me. I waited until I felt a connection with them—a little rush of aliveness in my heart center. Then without using my voice I told the coyotes I had food for them and asked them to appear. Within one minute, a coyote came over the ridge. He told the others, and the next day, two coyotes came over the slope. The next day there were four. This is when I stopped! I didn't want to endanger their lives by teaching them to trust humans, nor did I want to feed a pack of coyotes every day.

I did continue to feed one injured male who was partially bald from mange[12] and had bulging ribs. His right hind leg seemed to be broken, and he tucked it up skipping along on his remaining three limbs. He could not hunt food for himself. I had developed a relationship of trust with the coyote, who I named Kady. He and his buddy would appear as soon as I mentally announced my arrival, even though I never arrived at the park at the same time and sometimes skipped a day or two. For three weeks I fed him at our special, secluded spot while his buddy hung out and waited until Kady finished eating. Then he would escort Kady back over the hill.

---

[12] Many coyotes in Griffith Park were susceptible to mange, due to compromised immune systems, caused from eating ground squirrels which are routinely poisoned.

I then found Kathryn, a local, licensed, rehabilitation and rescue woman, who said she would take Kady and nurse him back to health. Together we set traps baited with raw meat, but the coyote was too smart and, as hungry as he was, he would not enter the traps for the food. Determined to outsmart Kady, Kathryn had planned to set a different type of trap, when the City became involved. They tied Kathryn's hands with a laundry list of paperwork to present, meetings to attend and demands to be met. They set their own traps—the same type which had not worked for us—and patrolled the area, which kept Kady, and all the coyotes, away. And which also made it difficult for me to leave food. It was illegal to feed wildlife. After a few weeks the City gave up.

I arrived at the park and mentally projected my arrival to Kady, but Kady's buddy came over the hill alone. I never saw my coyote friend again. Kathryn and I had come so close to helping him. But Kady apparently could not survive those last few weeks on his own.

Believe animals can hear you. Smokey was a feral cat in my backyard that the owner, Michael, had been feeding for twelve years. I began feeding her when Michael was traveling for two weeks. On the third day, Smokey didn't come out to eat. Worried, I mentally projected these words to her, "Smokey girl, why aren't you eating this morning? Are you all right?"

My interpretation of her thoughts went something like this:

"Not hungry. Ate a mouse last night."

Did a coyote get you?

"Nope. Too smart for that."

I asked her to please let me see her. She did not have to eat, but would she please just come out and show me that she was all right? My eyes were still closed when Smokey rustled out of the bushes, ran to me, and made eye contact before she circled her food bowl twice and ran back into hiding.

Finally, I put my beliefs to the test. I connected to her again before vacating the premises of my garden apartment. I didn't want to leave her behind. I sent Smokey images of an empty apartment stripped of furniture and animals, and her sitting alone in the yard with an empty food bowl. I then held an image in my mind of picking her up, placing her in the carrier and taking her with me. It was her choice. Did she want to be part of my family? Did she prefer to stay behind and fend for herself?

Smokey hung around near my patio garden bench—something she had never done before. I took this to be a yes, although I was not certain. Then came the final day and the test of my ultimate belief in my abilities. Smokey walked into the empty apartment. I closed the front door, placed the carrier in a vertical position and fully opened the carrier door. I mentally pictured her going in feet first. Then I sent her a contrasting image of her resisting and staying behind.

The last thing I wanted was to be torn up! Here was a twelve-year-old feral cat who had never been touched by humans. Here was a human who never thought to wear protective gloves or throw a towel around her. Without thinking, I bent over, placed my hands around her body and lifted her in the air. To my surprise, Smokey turned into a limp rag! All the way from beginning to end, she was easier to drop into the carrier than any domestic cat I had ever had. Miss Smokey-Girl Jones has been with me for five years and is almost twenty years old. She sleeps with me, allows me to pick her up for hugs, and wakes me up in the morning.

Telepathic communication has worked the same way with rats, lizards, and birds brought in by my cats as well as injured skunks and squirrels I found in the street. Mentally, I explained my intentions to help and told them their options. Then, with pure loving intentions—in total belief and confidence that they understood—I picked these animals up with my bare hands. Not one resisted or tried to bite. Even a baby lizard, suffering with feet, chin, and tail flattened in a glue trap, never struggled once against my rescue efforts, which lasted one hour. Telepathy has worked with bees and flies trapped in the house who immediately flew to the screen door when I telepathically told them I would release them outside. It has worked with wild birds who were trapped inside buildings.

When you believe in yourself and approach another living being with clear intention, fear drops away, and they return the trust. You meet them on common ground: love. I'll admit, my belief is not strong enough yet to handle a tiger. We all have our limitations.

Helen wrote to say that her little psychic feline friend, Billy, had acted strangely one day. Anxious at her heels, Billy didn't want Helen to leave the house. She described fear and despair in her cat's eyes, and said she heard the word "grenades." The following day, there was a bomb threat at the FBI building near her home. "Animals do really talk to you, if you listen," Helen said. "The emotions are easy to read." Helen heard Billy's thoughts—even though she had never taken an animal communication class.

If you are close to your companions, you are already hearing them, even if you don't realize it. It takes practice to differentiate their thoughts from your own. Your companion's thoughts can be as subtle as a breeze and may appear like your own thoughts.

I had spent my days painting outdoors at Jason's home while caring for Sanda, his German Shepherd. As usual, I was fully engrossed in the vibrancy of the garden and the colors on the canvas. Out of nowhere, the thought of taking Sanda for a walk flashed through my mind. I glanced up and to the right, where I had felt someone staring at me. Grinning and wide eyed, Sanda was standing at the front gate waiting for my answer.

Sometimes the messages from our animals are inspirational. Margaret, my artist friend, said that her dog, Hattie, knew exactly how to communicate with her whenever she was pondering on which direction her work should take. During the editing process of one of her videos, Hattie walked up to Margaret's computer and rested her head on Margaret's desk. The very next photo that appeared on the computer screen was the perfect image. It even contained Margaret's birthdate, which became the spin for her next still-photo series. Perhaps the perfect photo appeared to Margaret at the moment she consciously relaxed and let go. Our animals provide this space for us. I didn't need to convince Margaret that this was no coincidence. She instantly knew where her inspiration came from.

Listen to your thoughts! Believe in your abilities. Believe your animals can hear you. Most of all, believe that you can hear them.

3. Set Your Intention

Intention does not mean forcing your will, but holding your purpose or desire gently, allowing and trusting it will be done. Before a session—especially a healing or lost animal session—I imagine going out through the crown chakra to the Creator (or the upper worlds in Shamanic journeying). I say, "Father Mother God, Creator of all there is... it is my intention to receive information from (animal's name). Show me what I need to see. Tell me what I need to hear. Thank you. It is done." I will also do this when asking what vitamin or supplement an animal needs, or whenever I need any sort of additional information that I have not gotten from the animal.

After I project my thoughts, intentions and requests into infinity, I empty myself of expectations and stay open to receive.

Saying "it is done" is important. We intend to receive or manifest whatever it is, knowing that the desired object is already here or that the task, animal connection, or healing is already completed. This is different from wanting, wishing, or hoping, which imparts to the universe that we are lacking and sets us apart from the result. Wanting is a weak mindset that sends wish-wash to the universe. Instead, know that you are always connected to and co-creating with the Field of Intelligence, not groping in a sea of separateness. Dr. Wayne Dyer says, "When you become one with intention, you're transcending the ego-mind and becoming the universal all-creative mind."

Quantum physics has proven that intention sets thought in motion. The universe sends back what we bring forth. We don't need to wait to set intentions on New Year's Eve. Just as a golfer sees the ball falling into the hole and a cat becomes one with the prey before the capture, see yourself talking to and hearing animals. Set your intention to do so. Know that it is done.

4. See Animals As Equal

If we think we are superior in any way, we will shut down the natural flow of communication and limit our receptivity. Then our animals may be reluctant to open up. See your animals as companions, family members, and friends—not as pets. Consider their feelings, fears, and comforts. No doubt you already do, or you would have had no interest in reading this book.

Remember that we are not our animal's owner. We are their caretakers or guardians. We cannot own a living being. Yet because animals are, for the most part, still considered property, they do not have equal rights. Activists and vegans are the voice for animals, raising consciousness and changing the way in which we view and treat animals. Animals are sentient beings with purposes of their own. They have emotional and spiritual lives, friends, family, fears, and concerns. They and all living beings cherish their lives, just as we do ours. Factory farming in America is a holocaust, and yet we turn a blind eye to the horror. We would never allow our cats, dogs, and horses to endure these atrocities so we can have hamburgers and handbags. Yet we allow it to happen to other beings.

Maple Sugar

I knew that animals in factory production were genetically bred to unnatural proportions to increase "meat" production, but the consequences of this reality hadn't really sunk in until I met Jumper, a female pig at the Farm Sanctuary[13] in Acton, California.

I visited the twenty-six acre sanctuary that day with other activists. Among them were the director of the Museum of Animals and Society in Los Angeles; a man from Animals Asia—an organization that works to end bear bile farming, a painful and invasive procedure in which caged bears are "milked" for their bile in China and Vietnam; and an animal activist and investigative photojournalist from Canada.

A sweet, fragrant scent wafted through the barn as I stepped through thick mounds of hay to sit next to Jumper. Jumper was the shocking size of a small cow—close to eight-hundred pounds. (The factory-raised cows and steers who were brought to the sanctuary

---

[13]   Visit this website to learn how we treat the animals we eat: www.farmsanctuary.org

were disproportionately enormous as well.) The natural weight of a pig in the wild is one-hundred to two-hundred pounds. Some of the pigs here weighed almost one-thousand pounds. Of course pigs don't get this large while they are in the animal factories, because they are killed at five months of age. But even at this young age, pigs, as well as chickens, are bred to grow so fast that their legs cannot support their own weight. I watched Jumper's barn-mates struggling to stand on their legs. Eventually three of her mates went outdoors to sun themselves. Jumper stayed behind.

The staff had told us that Jumper was "fat blind"— another impairment caused from the manipulated weight gain. But according to Jumper, she was not yet entirely blind. Without anyone knowing it, I had a silent conversation with her. She told me she preferred to stay inside the cool, dark barn and venture outdoors in the early morning hours or at dusk. She said the bright sun hurt her eyes.

Other pigs, like Sabrina, were not as friendly to humans. We were told to stand on the opposite side of the fence while visiting Sabrina. Although she was relaxed and cared for at the sanctuary now, she carried an aura of sadness. She, like the other female pigs and dairy cows, had been forced to give birth repeatedly, only to see and hear every one of her babies later being slaughtered. The mothers mourn for years. Sabrina had undoubtedly spent her life laying on her side in a gestation crate—a space so small that did not allow the sow to even turn her head to see her babies nursing through the bars of the crate. Like chickens and male calves,[14] the sows had no room to even turn around or stand up.

I had felt the excruciating pain in my own body while not moving a muscle during a four-hour meditation sit. I had finally shifted my legs after two hours. What was it like to not move a muscle for our entire lives? Why did we inflict this pain upon innocent animals simply for our appetites?

Visiting the animals at the sanctuary was both delightful and sad. What still lingers in my mind is that pleasant, sugary scented barn. I assumed this smell came from the generous amount of hay that covered the floor. The photojournalist had grinned at me and said what she loved most about pigs was that smell of maple sugar. This fragrance that permeated the barn came from their naturally sweet body odor.

How could we not see the intelligence and sweetness of all animals? There is a disconnect and a blindfold across our dinner tables. All animals have the right to a decent life. All beings wish to live. All of us have emotions, feel pain and grieve.

Animals will open up to us when we are truly humble, sincere and loving toward them. And when we truly see them as equals.

Spiders Are Mothers Too

I look before blasting the shower, although one morning I startled an almost invisible adolescent daddy-longlegs. I felt his terror as he

---

[14] Veal calves are severely restrained in tiny, dark crates to prohibit muscle growth, and are fed a milk substitute low in iron to make them anemic, in order to produce tender "veal." As many as twenty-thousand chickens are crammed into a warehouse. Each bird has a space slightly larger than a sheet of letter-size paper. www.farmsanctuary.org

ran frantically to hide. I picked him up with a tissue for release on the bathroom floor, but a string of silk still attached to him sent him swinging back toward my body. I had already turned on the water for the second time when I noticed the little creature again. His head was bent, and he walked backward in circles. I had accidentally crippled him.

It occurred to me to put him in the corner of the bathroom floor, about six inches below a much bigger daddy-longlegs. I thought she might help him. The next time I looked, the big spider had brought the adolescent to her body and formed a canopy of lanky legs around him. One leg was bent inward like an elbow, and she rocked back and forth, to and from the small spider, with the elbow of that one bent leg aimed at his head. It looked as though she was either healing or mercy-killing him. Several hours later, she held his head right up against her body. The next day, he was flat dead against the wall and she was nowhere to be seen.

Insects and spiders have communication skills as complex as any other species. Scientists who study insect and spider behavior have found that they recognize their nest mates and parents. Adults recognize the opposite sex and engage in courtship and mating. They give off alarms to warn one another of danger.

Did the motherly spider see the adolescent as food?[15] Could she have known that the injured adolescent could not have survived on his own, and therefore put him out of his misery? Are insects and spiders capable of feeling compassion? I don't know, but I invite us all to stay open to possibilities, and to perhaps have second thoughts before we step on insects or blast them with poison.

---

[15]   Daddy longlegs are said to be cannibalistic—eating each other if food is scarce. On the other hand, it is said that females are excellent mothers, who carry their eggs in their mouths and feed their young. http://www.naturespot.org.uk

I believe that all beings share an equal right to life regardless of whether we believe they are capable of feeling compassion, whether we believe they have thoughts or emotions, and whether their life span is one day. All creatures cherish their lives, and all life is aware and communicating.

Mother Tree

The desert can quell our busy minds. The landscape thrives in stillness and aliveness, and holds a healing, peaceful presence for all who pass through. I was on my fifth day of silence during another Buddhist retreat at Joshua Tree, located in the California High Desert. Graceful cranes, desert tortoises, roadrunners and jackrabbits appeared on my daily walks. Every animal who showed up reminded me that I was a welcomed visitor in their home. In gratitude, I wrapped my arms around a young Joshua tree.

The upper trunk, covered with ten-inch draping quills, was not brittle as I expected it to be, but felt like a padded blanket against my cheek. Ever so subtlety, the trunk gently rocked when the wind blew. I felt a soothing, relaxed coolness in my solar plexus. I wondered if the tree emitted a coolness to withstand the desert heat, or if the coolness resulted from the fifty-two degree temperature from the previous evening. I had hugged the tree just shortly after dawn.

I decided to hug another larger Joshua tree at six-thirty in the evening, after it had stood all day in the sweltering sun. After pressing myself against its trunk for a while, I felt the same calming coolness in my solar plexus, and I held on. Coolness was an integral part of the Joshua tree. This big fellow, however, had a completely different signature than the young tree had. It felt expansive, solid and nurturing, and as it rocked me with the wind, I felt as if I were cradled in a mother's arms.

When we see all living beings as equal and no different from ourselves, our relationship with animals and all life will deepen.

5. Trust Yourself

Resting under a spruce tree in Pennsylvania, I heard these words, "Relax more. Flow like the wind. Circles. Let your mind move in circles. Be guided. Do not lead your thoughts. Move and connect." Wonderful wisdom words: move and connect. Tap into the flow of the Creative Intelligence that governs the universe—the present moment. Do not lead your thoughts or let them lead you. Surrender, remain open, circulate your energy and receive. Become like water and allow yourself to be directed. This is what trees do. Simply be and observe, like them.

I stand in the wind. Look at my leaves. Not one moves in the same direction. But all move together. A quantum physics theory from a tree? I had stood on a mountain top under a eucalyptus tree on the windy afternoon when I heard that thought.

Trees are wise, gentle, magnificent beings and the most spiritually advanced of the plant kingdom. It is said that they are always in meditation. When we get out of our heads and drop down to our bodies, we can experience their majesty, neutrality and calmness, and hear their wisdom.

Everything is alive and conscious. The Divine Intelligence is always speaking through us, through all forms, even inanimate forms. I got such guidance when I asked for help to find my missing cat, Giovanni.

Having exhausted all my search efforts, I asked a colleague for help. She advised me to ask for a neon sign. I told her I had already asked for signs and had received nothing. She said, "No. Not just a sign. A NEON sign. Something huge to hit you over the head." So I asked for a neon sign.

The next day I drove, half-dazed, through the San Fernando Valley. Suddenly, something pulled my attention to the left. In front of a thrift store was a huge sign on the ground; it was neon, and it was lit up. It read, TRUST GOD. I ended my search for Giovanni. I never found him, but I knew deep in my heart that, whether alive in his physical body or in spirit, he was safe in his journey.

If you don't believe in signs, then call it synchronicity. Call it whatever you'd like. Just stay open to receive. Pay attention. Be observant and aware with all your senses when asking the universe a question. Everything is your answer. We are not alone in life or in death. Always trust the information that you get—whether you hear it from a bird, horse, lizard, oak tree, or even blowing in the wind. All life is connected and communicating.

Consider Hawthorn

When I awoke one morning, I recalled those words in a dream. I had no idea for whom I should consider hawthorn or what it was even used for. I then read that hawthorn was good for heart problems, diabetes and high blood pressure. My Dad had all three! So I bought the herb, and he started taking it. I trusted my dream, and my Dad trusted me. Although his doctors were leery and hard to convince, they finally added hawthorn to his list of medications and supplements. Of course, I never told the doctors I dreamt it up! The herb, along with dietary changes, seemed to lower my dad's high sugar levels, and he never needed high doses of medication.

The universal mind speaks in pictures, and our dreams are often packed with visual symbolism. In another dream, my friend's wife, who I barely knew, showed me a medicinal substance in a bottle and told me this would help my cat's kidneys. I saw the label on the bottle clearly. When I woke up, I remembered the dream and immediately went online to research the name I had read on the label. It turned out to be a Chinese herbal remedy, which I bought for my cat Bubby. I had no idea why my friend's wife was the one who showed up in the dream. It later dawned on me that my friend's wife was Chinese.

Listen to your dreams. Stay awake. See everyone as a mirror. Always trust the thoughts, images and feelings that enter your mind. Don't discount anything. If you feel sadness when you look at your companions, you are most likely receiving this from them. Get out of your mind and drop down to your heart. Set your intention to do so. Animal communication is a heart-centered language. If you still are not certain what the animal is trying to convey, drop down to the Nabi chakra—the area three finger-widths below the navel—and feel the answer in your gut.

A two-month-old kitten would have suffocated if I had not trusted what I received from his litter mate. Although he was also only two months old, he knew his sister was in danger! I took care of a friend's two dogs, two cats, and a litter of six black-and-white tuxedo kittens (yes, I told her to spay her cat)! While I was doing the dishes, this one little guy mewed nonstop to get my attention. I asked him what was wrong, although my attention was on finishing my dish washing. Finally, when the dishes were done, I looked at the noisy kitten, dropped down to my heart center and asked again what was wrong. This time, I closed my eyes so I could hear. He sent me an image of his tiny sister in the refrigerator! I immediately yanked the refrigerator door wide open, and sure enough, his sister came tumbling out—alive.

Cultivating Big Cat Awareness

I volunteered for two years at a wildlife sanctuary, located near Los Angeles. I looked forward to the time I spent with the chimpanzees, and with Jeffery in particular, a thirty-four year old chimp who liked to wear our sun glasses, finger-paint, and dance when we beat the conga drum for him. It was sad to think that these chimps had been people's "pets." Now, having grown too big and dangerous to be kept in a home, they would spend the rest of their lives in captivity. It was even more disturbing that the retired laboratory chimpanzees at the sanctuary had to be kept isolated from everyone. They hated humans. But at least now they could live the rest of their lives unharmed—unlike many other chimps, some approaching fifty years of age, who will never see daylight or leave their small, isolated cages in the laboratories. We weren't supposed to get too physically close to any of the animals for safety reasons, but when no one was looking Jeffery would pucker-up his face against the cage, and I would kiss him on his soft, plump lips.

The biggest treat was when Niko walked the lions and tigers on a leash. As he approached with the big cats, he would yell to anyone in his view, "Get out of the way. NOW." And the humans, entrained to his voice, would scamper away like overgrown puppies to clear the pathway for the big cats to glide through.

One time I ignored Niko and decided not to move. I hid in the bushes, about fifteen feet below the path, so that I could get a close look at Paradise, the majestic lioness, as she strode past. Crouched as still as a mouse, and peeking through a camouflage of thick shrubs, I was awestruck at the magnitude of her beauty and grace as the lioness sauntered past me. Suddenly Paradise, who was already now at least fifty feet beyond me, halted to a complete stop. In a quick second she swung her head around and locked her eyes on me. The curious lioness strutted toward me. Paradise caught me with my hands in the cookie jar, and Niko nearly killed me for being there.

Several yards away the lioness had felt my eyes on her and sensed my presence behind her back. She sized me up in one split second. Animals, both wild and domestic, are watching us all the time. They see us even when we don't see them. I can sit in the park all day and think that I am alone, until I throw a piece of bread on the ground for a squirrel. Suddenly a flock of sparrows swoop down, coyotes appear from nowhere, and ravens dive-bomb their competition.

Animals walk tuned-in to their environment. Fully alive in their bodies, they remain alert in the outside world while navigating from the still point within. Always present in their surroundings, animals feel the vibrational frequencies of other animals, predators and humans— even miles away—and hear every sound and see every movement around, above and below them. And, like the lioness, it seems that all animals have a third eye behind their heads. Animals have to develop this inclusive web of awareness. They know that if they are not aware one-hundred percent of the time, they put their lives in danger.

We can learn from the animals and practice their skills. When we become one with our environment and wake up to the natural world around us, nothing is a distraction, nothing is overlooked, life becomes magical and animals begin to trust us.

We want to cultivate a Paradise awareness when we communicate to animals. Develop an around-the-bend consciousness and move out of our tunnel vision. We can merge with an animal's thoughts while remaining alert to all the sensory data flowing in. We can get out of our chatter and notice what we focus on. We can notice what our senses are taking in, and trust ourselves and trust the information that we have felt, seen, heard and received. Animals don't doubt their instincts. They live in their bodies, and they don't like it when we're lost in thought. Trust, and becoming mindful of life around us, will increase our awareness and build our self-confidence.

Become aware of the subtle pictures and thoughts in your mind and of every feeling in your body. Allow yourself to feel more deeply with an open heart and less fear. Make this your daily practice. Remember that our bodies are also like radar. We send and receive information to and from one another, and to and from our animals, all the time. Thoughts are like radio waves that are broadcast far and wide. We just need to fine-tune our channel to pick up the radio waves.

Indigenous cultures relied upon the intuition to track an animal in the wilderness. They became quiet and, attuned to the physical sensations in their body, they followed the direction that they were drawn toward. No doubt they also attuned themselves with the frequency of the animal.

I once "tracked" a lost animal in this way. I wasn't in the forest, but smack in the city of Los Angeles. Sanda, the German Shepherd I was caring for, had disappeared from her yard one afternoon. She had been missing now for a few days, and I had no idea where to start looking. New to telepathic communication at the time, I unknowingly applied two essentials of telepathy to find Sanda—surrendering (allowing and listening, instead of forcing my will or resisting what is) and solely trusting my intuition.

After making a telepathic connection with her, I got into my car, dropped down to the heart center and set my intention by saying, "Guide me to Sanda." I relaxed and began driving with no destination in mind. While traveling alongside the Metro rail, near a busy intersection in Los Angeles, I heard the little voice inside instructing me to turn left. Without doubt, I turned left and kept driving up this winding street, which narrowed into the hills and ended at a dirt road. Just then the intellect kicked in, and I heard myself thinking, *"This is ridiculous. She wouldn't have gone this far and certainly not down this bumpy, dirt road. Turn around and go back."* This made total sense. The road was at least two miles from her home, and Sanda had bad hips. She could not have possibly walked this far.

However, trusting one's gut will seldom make sense to the intellect. This is precisely why we put logic aside, keep our antennae out, surrender and follow our intuition. This is called... trust.

Ignoring logic, I listened to the small inner voice which then said, "Keep going down the dirt road." I drove over the bumps, and drove over my doubts, while logic rebelled and yapped away in disregard, *"What am I doing? This is dumb. She's not here. I'm wasting time."* Again the voice piped in. "Keep driving." I continued to drive down the narrow dirt road when suddenly up ahead, moving toward my direction, was a man and woman walking two dogs. I thought I was dreaming. As they got closer I recognized Sanda, and Sanda recognized me. I called out to her in shock and disbelief, and in awe of my invisible helper, the little friend inside, who reunited me with Sanda. I ran to her, and we embraced like two long-lost lovers on the lonely road.

The kind couple had found Sanda lost in the street not too far from her home. It took thirty minutes for them to coax her into their car. They read her address on her tags, and they had left a note on the backside of an advertisement and slipped it in the mail box. I never saw the note. I saw the advertisement and tossed it in the trash.

Often times it is not what we do, but what we don't do that brings results. Practice letting go. You are already hearing your animals, and when you drop down, get out of your head, and rest in yourself, you will feel the heart connection and you will know that you are hearing them.

Trust your intuition and enjoy the ride!

AUTHOR AFTERTHOUGHTS

As Maharaji said, "No one dies before their time or stays one moment after." I believe our lives are Divinely timed. There are no coincidences or accidents. I knew. I felt. I had an earth-shattering premonition the day before my cat, Ku Ku, was killed by a car. An accident? How did I pick up on the impending event if it wasn't already in motion?

Was Ku Ku's death merely a random act of being in the wrong place at the wrong time? Perhaps we always have our feet in the correct place, no matter where we stand. When we stay tuned, we tap into the momentum of unfolding possibilities. Yet there are many possibilities. And whatever possibility we choose has consequences, for us and others.

Physicists have found that when they tried to observe a quantum wave of energy, it changed into a particle (matter). This means that where we place our consciousness or focus our attention (what we observe), becomes what we manifest in our life. In the words of Lynne McTaggart, author, researcher and lecturer, reality is like unset Jell-O. It is our consciousness that sets the random quantum waves of energy into particles or form. We create our experiences (our reality) with our thoughts. Reality, therefore, is a reflection of our thought forms and an external manifestation of our inner world. There will always be war until each and every one of us realizes and works on our own violent thoughts, fears and beliefs in lack. Peace begins from the inside out.

Once, while reading a book in bed, I suddenly left my body. I was strangely positioned in the top corner of the room watching myself below holding the book. Who was watching me? How could I be both here and there at once? Who was I? I could see myself sitting on the bed, but I could no longer see the text on the pages of the book until I popped back into my body, which then felt dense and concentrated in comparison. After my out of body experience, I knew that it was possible to see without the physical eyes. I realized that we are not our bodies. We are not our thoughts. We are consciousness, and where we project our consciousness will determine our experiences.

My father was radiant when he lay dying in bed. I watched him sleep. His face danced with grins while he occasionally arched his eyebrows and nodded his head. His lips shaped silent words and his tongue moved in his mouth with the dialogue he must have entertained in his mind. Who was he talking to? His arms gently waved in front of him as he reached out to invisible friends and helpers. They were present in the room, present in his mind and probably there to help him cross over. I felt the strong presence of many in the room. Then he slipped back into body consciousness, opened his eyes and giggled when he saw me. He said he could recall an incident in his youth—a memory of a friend or an event in his life—and then instantly be there with all his five senses, and that it was as real as my presence with him in the room.

Then, with feet in both worlds, he closed his eyes again and dove back into the Matrix Field. He was consciously creating his experiences. My Dad gently set his intention to be wherever he chose to be.

We're always creating our experiences, and we can become more conscious of it. Perhaps when we approach death, we are more aware that we set the Jell-O. The ego is blasted away, and we are not bogged down in dense bodies or in the illusion of permanence or by the confines of our cemented beliefs. There are no boundaries when we step out of the flesh.

It may be that we set the Jell-O before we take birth. Do we decide, before body, to learn about compassion, for example—and then attract experiences or certain people or animals into our lives that will help us to grow our compassion and learn what we agreed to learn?

If we are all connected on a soul, energetic, and cellular level, our experiences may very well be Divinely timed for our spiritual growth. Perhaps we still learn what it is we need to learn, no matter which path we take or choice we make. Or maybe we choose from random possibilities and experience the fruit of our random choices. Either way, we can relax a bit. We can accept, trust the chaos, and process of life lessons that unfold. We can stop resisting what is, and stop seeing ourselves as victims. In the words of Byron Katie, "Everything happens *for* us, not *to* us." We drop the blame when we realize we are co-creating and believe that our thoughts do affect our circumstances.

Thoughts can change our lives and influence others, including our animals. If we know that we truly are one energy manifested in different forms, we treat ourselves and others with dignity, respect and love. If we are all connected, we forgive others, because we know we are forgiving ourselves. We know that what we do to others and to our planet, we do to ourselves.

When we are aware, we won't destroy the ozone layer, the rainforest, animals, or each other, because we understand our integration with all that is and the divinely designed cosmic web of which we are a part. We will view animals differently, seeing their souls and ourselves in their eyes. With awareness, we will extend our compassion not only to cats, dogs, hummingbirds, and horses but also to chickens, cows, pigs, and bats. We can respect the lives of both dolphins and tuna. All life is sacred, even the tiniest ant or the dirtiest rat.

No One Likes A Dirty Rat

It occurred to me that it had been a long time since I rescued an animal, and I hoped that I would not see one needing help on this day. Instantly, the universe responded to my thought, and I spotted a small animal in the middle of the road. The creature was smelling the ground and seemed oblivious to the sound of my horn. Damn. I just wanted to go home, but I pulled over.

It was a baby rat. I used my sweater to shoo him off the road, but he grabbed onto the sweater. When I picked him up, he squirmed hard, squealed, then tried to bite, so I dropped him and walked away. He followed me, ran up my leg, and I brushed him off with the sweater. Then he sprinted up my leg again, pattering along my jeans like a drizzle of rain.

This time I draped my sweater over him. He really liked the fuzzy mother warmth and sat still as a stone against my chest as I knocked on neighbor's doors. "Did anyone lose a pet rat?" Doors shut quickly when you are holding the bubonic plague. Confident that Rat Boy belonged to someone, I took him home intending to post signs the following day. I knew nothing about rats, but I was advised to make a nest of shredded paper, which I did, and to provide a bowl of water. I put him in the back of a cat carrier, hidden in the bathroom, away from the cats.

Rat Boy immediately ran to his newspaper bed. Then he balanced on the edge of the water bowl, drinking and drinking. But something was terribly wrong with Rat Boy. He swayed and breathed with a clicking sound. He would not eat one morsel of food.

That evening, I opened the carrier door. He came right out. This time he let me pick him up, and I put him on my lap. Light as a feather, he snuggled in the folds of my bathrobe as I did a telepathic communication for a client in Louisiana. Amy had lost her cat, Willy, and was beside herself.

When I tuned in to Willy, he told me he was close by, knew the way home, felt safe where he was, and did not feel brave enough to return. He showed me white lattice near a wall and himself lying on a porch. No, he said, he did not go down the drain pipe, as his person had thought. He had not followed the black and white kitty and hadn't even seen the gray cat that Amy was certain he was with. I had already told Amy to search nearby homes. Then I looked down at Rat Boy and told him that I would find his home. I asked him where he came from. Could he describe his house? He showed me a light blue house with red and pink roses around it. I watched him closely. His chest clicked and heaved with every inhale.

By morning, Rat Boy still wasn't eating, so I took him to an emergency animal clinic. After a long wait in dead silence, I was given odd, dirty looks and a grown-up scolding.

"This is not a pet. This is a real rat. You should have left him on the street. The vet is not comfortable treating him. You'll have to leave immediately. Wash your hands. Don't touch him or let him out of this carrier. Make sure your cats do not have contact with your clothes."

The tech went on and on about typhus bacterial infections, and how no one there wanted to get sick and die.

"Aren't you being a little dramatic?" I asked.

The staff was furious. "The best thing you can do for him is to take him to the shelter and have him euthanized. We will charge you too much money here. Please leave now."

They handed me back the carrier. They had taken off the screening I had wrapped around the carrier door to keep him in, and now Rat Boy panicked and was about to squeeze through the one-inch holes of the carrier door.

"He's coming out!" I alerted the staff as I reached to grab a Kleenex or magazine to block his little head. They screamed back. "DON'T TOUCH ANYTHING!"

Rat Boy and I slunk like two lepers through the waiting room, occupied with professed animal lovers who cringed as I walked past them. I contacted Kathryn, the rehab person who rescues wild rodents, squirrels, skunks, raccoons, opossum, and coyotes. She couldn't take him at the moment, but she said she thought Rat Boy was either an orphaned juvenile or had been poisoned.

Rat Boy was just a baby. No wonder his eyes lit up at my cat's furry rat toy I placed next to him. It was as big as his mother, and Rat Boy had scurried right up to it, stroked it and cozied up. I cut a piece of my terry-cloth bathrobe and covered them both. He loved sleeping with his fake mom in his dark, crispy nest.

I changed Rat Boy's food pellets to instant quinoa flakes, almond butter, and minced apple. Nothing enticed him. I called and left messages with three more wild rodent rehab people. No replies. Rat Boy still clicked away and swayed with each labored breath. Since I could find no one to help him, I decided to have him put down. But despite calling several vets and pleading for euthanasia, not one vet wanted him or me stepping foot into their clinics.

Finally, I found a vet who agreed to treat him. She ended up observing him two feet away, through a glass cage. She confirmed he had been poisoned but refused to euthanize him, and charged me the exotic pet fee. There was nothing exotic about Rat Boy. He was a street rat. I argued, but still had to pay the extra fee. I took him home and put him on my lap. I didn't think about typhus and death. I thought about a little orphaned juvenile who was poisoned, not seen for who he was and mistaken for a dirty rat.

At midnight, after four days of extensive searching, I found a vet at a wild life rehabilitation center in Long Beach willing to take him in the morning. But Rat Boy died next to his surrogate mom during the night. I held a ceremony, prayed, chanted and buried Rat Boy with the toy rat in the backyard.

Amy found Willy napping on the neighbor's porch near the white lattice. The house was light blue with red and pink roses around it— exactly like the house that Rat Boy had described to me. I have no rational or irrational explanation. I just know that the universe speaks through all forms. I know that rats are sweet, gentle, affectionate animals. And I know that if Rat Boy had been a white dove, the outcome would have been totally different.

Observe your mind. The only differences between species are in your own thoughts. Notice the fear and the feelings that arise to create boundaries between you. All living beings are manifestations of the same life force. And every animal has a unique personality. See all animals as equal. Before anyone thinks of poisoning an animal, remember one thing. It hurts—for a long time.

Animal communication is the groundwork that makes communication with all life possible. It is a revolutionary approach to opening our hearts and changing our lives for the better. When we take the time to heighten and develop our own innate abilities, we trust our knowing, see the subtle shades of meaning, understand with empathy and listen with compassion. We no longer operate from the ego, but from the Divine Wisdom within. We tap into the stream of consciousness where the animals reside, in present awareness, and cultivate a more conscious way of interpreting and relating to the world around us. When we develop our compassion, our pain will not stem from our own concerns but from our kinship with all living beings.

Animals are great teachers of impermanence—here for a handful of time—who show us how to allow and let go. For me, they have been the greatest inspiration and models of patience, forgiveness, kindness, generosity, peace, love, compassion and spontaneity—things that can take us lifetimes to learn and things that I am continuously learning.

Long live the animals in our hearts and who share our planet. They come as spiritual friends and have taught us for lifetimes. Are we ready to listen?

THE FUR, FEATHER AND COLD-BLOODED MANIFESTO

Let us see our animals for who they are.

Let us know their purpose in our lives.

Let us understand the root cause of their problems.

Let us invite them into our hearts.

Let us hear that which they try to tell us.

Let us consider the life lessons of our lives together.

Let us drop our human superiority.

Let us touch them with kindness.

Let us see all animals as equal and help to end their suffering.

Let us accept the gifts they bring us, and the blessings they leave behind.

*

May all beings be happy.
May all my thoughts, words and actions
contribute in some way to the happiness of all beings.

Thich Nhat Hanh

THE BLESSINGS

W e can develop the pituitary and pineal glands, located in the brain. The pituitary gland is located behind the forehead, between the eyes. The pineal gland is just above and behind it. Also referred to as the Third Eye, Seat of the Soul, or Seat of Illumination, the pineal gland is a gateway to the higher spiritual frequencies and experiences of oneness. The pranayama, or breath awareness, that you will learn in the following two meditations energizes the body and quiets and clarifies the mind. The eye position you will be shown engages the optic nerve, which stimulates both the pituitary and pineal glands and the frontal lobe of the brain. Yogis say that, when both glands are stimulated, the Third Eye—also known as the All-Seeing Eye—is activated. When these higher centers of the brain are activated, our clairvoyant abilities and claircognizance can develop.

The following two gifts can be downloaded from my website. A password will be given to you when you enter your email address.

Blessing #1: Quieting the Mind

This grounding, guided meditation is based on Zen sitting mediation, or Zazen. This method, practiced for more than 2,000 years, will help quiet and focus the mind, develop concentration, and increase your inner listening and intuition. In the beginning, you will notice the activity in your mind. You will learn ways to quiet the mind and remain present. Eventually, you will learn to integrate external sounds, noise and uncomfortable body sensations. You will be able to incorporate pain in the body, and anything else you normally consider a distraction, into your meditation.

Everything is your experience. Nothing is excluded. This type of meditation is a practice of presence, staying in your body, observing your thoughts and allowing them to come into your mind without attaching to them. It is a meditation on mindfulness, on watching the mind-states that arise, and your reactions to both internal and external stimuli. With practice, your mind will become more still and peaceful and you will be able to "see" your thoughts and decide whether you want to think them or not. We do have a choice. Meditating every day with this method has numerous benefits, one being that our pituitary and pineal glands are stimulated, opening our psychic centers. This meditation also helps to still the chatter in the mind so we can begin to hear our animal's thoughts, and learn to distinguish their thoughts from our own. This recording comes with a .pdf file demonstrating and explaining the body and hand postures.

Blessing #2: Meditation To Increase Intuition

In this video, I demonstrate a Kundalini Yoga pranayam (breathing meditation exercise) that develops the pituitary gland, stimulates the pineal gland and increases our intuition. Yogi Bhajan suggests we do this seven minutes a day for forty days. When an activity is repeated for forty consecutive days, new pathways are created in the brain. This video comes with a .pdf file of a list of foods that may help stimulate the pineal gland.

CONTACT INFORMATION

To find out more about consultations, workshops and seminars, Animal Communication retreats and speaking events, or to receive your two free audio and video downloads, please visit Diana DelMonte's main website: www.DianaDelMonte.com.

The website offers a schedule of upcoming events, information about locating lost animals, recorded meditations for missing animals and animals in transition, audio versions of both Diana's books and other services. You'll also find articles by Diana, interviews, videos about animal communication, book trailers, and past seminar retreats.

For healing sessions (for humans) or to read about Diana's healing work, please visit www.DianaHealer.com.

For consultations or media requests, please e-mail or call the phone number posted on the website.

Remember to access your gifts by signing-in to Diana's website, and entering the password.

BIBLIOGRAPHY

The Field, Lynne McTaggart

The Intention Experiment, Lynne McTaggart

The Holographic Universe, Michael Talbot

The Divine Matrix, Gregg Bradin

The Biology of Belief, Bruce Lipton

*Dogs That Know When Their Owners Are Coming Home,
    And Other Unexplained Powers Of Animals*, Rupert Sheldrake

The Shift: The Revolution In Human Consciousness, Owen Waters

Remote Viewing, David Moorehouse

Mind Body Code, Dr. Mario Martinez

The Souls of Animals, Gary Kowalski

The Master's Touch: On Being A Sacred Teacher For The New Age,
    Yogi Bhajan, Ph.D.

The Living Matrix: A Film On The New Science Of Healing, Greg
    Becker and Harry Massey

The Power of Intention, Dr. Wayne Dyer

Love, Medicine and Miracles, The Art of Healing, Bernie Siegel, M.D.

You Can Heal Your Life, Louise Hay

The Miracle of Mindfulness, Thich Nhat Hanh

Kinship with All Life, Allan Boone